How To Use

HAND

AND

POWER

TOOLS

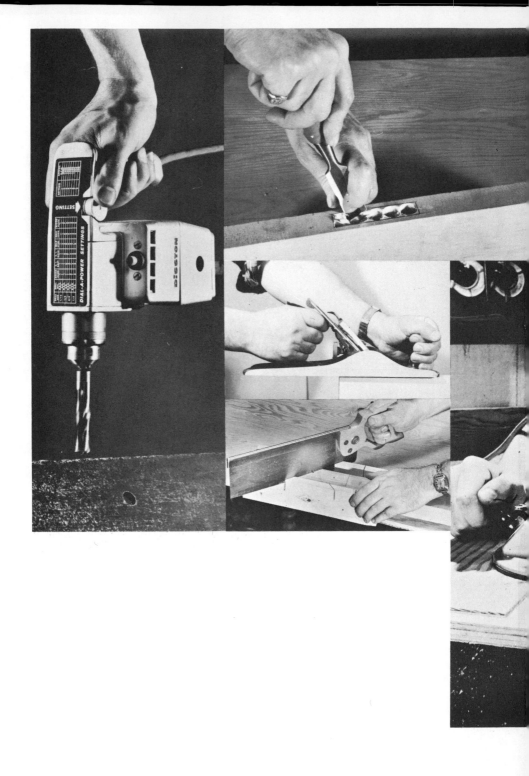

How To Use
HAND
AND
POWER
TOOLS

By
GEORGE DANIELS

Popular Science • Harper & Row
New York, Evanston, San Francisco, London

Library of Congress Catalog Card Number: 64-13135
ISBN: 0-06-010956-4

First Edition, 1964
Thirteen Printings

Second Edition, Revised and Updated, 1976

Seventh Printing, 1978

Manufactured in the United States of America

CONTENTS

Part I—HAND TOOLS

1. Early Tool Lore   7
2. Tools for Measuring and Marking   12
3. Saws   22
4. Chisels   31
5. Planes   38
6. Tools for Boring Holes   45
7. Hammers   54
8. Screwdrivers   60
9. Files and Rasps   63
10. Glues and Clamps   69
11. Coated Abrasives   77

Part II—POWER TOOLS

12. Planning the Power Tool Shop   82
13. The Portable Power Drill   86
14. The Sabre Saw   93

15. The Portable Circular Saw   101

16. Power Sanders   106

17. The Router   112

18. The Table Saw   118

19. The Radial-Arm Saw   130

20. The Drill Press   137

21. Lathes   144

22. The Jointer   153

23. Tools for Delicate Work   155

Index   157

Part I

CHAPTER ONE

EARLY TOOL LORE

IN THE BACKGROUND of almost every tool you use, and some you don't, there's a story or two. Even the innocuous measuring tools in the following chapter have had their exciting moments. Simply owning a yardstick could have landed you in a French jail during the 1790s. The government pushed the metric system with such fervor that inches, feet, and yards were outlawed and spies helped police track down anyone using them. Carpenters of the era actually had to figure their working time on the basis of a metric day with ten hours of 100 minutes of 100 seconds. Not surprisingly, the leader of the metric committee ended his career on the guillotine.

Our non-metric rules had a less dramatic but equally confusing past. The inch was the invention of the Romans, who called it a thumb breadth. England's King Edward II decreed it was the length of three barleycorns laid end to end. For "accuracy" the barleycorns were later divided into four poppy seeds apiece, and each poppy seed into twelve human hairs. King Henry I added another touch by fixing the yard as the distance from the end of his nose to the tip of his thumb. And to top it all off, the rod, as a measuring unit, was established as the total length of the *left* feet of the first sixteen men to come out of a specified church on a particular Sunday. It turned out to be 16½′ and it's the same today. So when you use your measuring tools be glad the groundwork has been completed.

Sometimes there is a story in the name of a tool. The Butcher saw which is used in your meat market resembles an oversized hacksaw, and it's an indispensable tool of the trade. Yet it gets its name not from its use but from its Irish inventor of long ago, Dr. R. G. Butcher, who developed it for *bone surgery*. The hole saw, too, had a surgical start. Today, you might use it to cut a gauge hole in an instrument panel. In smaller form it was an early tool for opening the human skull. Delve into the saw's past and you'll find other surprises; one of the first major patents on the bandsaw was issued to a woman—in France—where more romantic considerations usually supersede machine tools in the feminine mind.

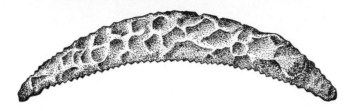

This neatly-toothed flint saw, made by Neanderthal man, has a curved blade similar to today's pruning saw.

We can only guess how long saws have been with us, but we have a few samples of neatly toothed flint models made by Neanderthal men 130,000 years ago. Some have a blade plan that almost matches today's pruning saws and they're still usable. Even inserted-tooth saws like modern industry's diamond-tipped forms are an old story. Teeth of ancient Egyptian and Inca stone-cutting saws were tipped with such exotic jewels as diamonds and emeralds. Lacking a ready jewel supply, Tahitian sawyers of the distant past used an interesting substitute—shark's teeth.

All along the line, traditional saw design has been slow to change. The oldest Oriental and Egyptian saws ever found had teeth pointing backward to cut on the pull stroke. And in much of the Orient saw teeth still point and cut the same way. In the West, where all hand saws but the coping saw cut on the push stroke, some odd features have persisted. For decades many of our saws had a small nib projecting at the top of the blade tip. It was some-times called a "sight," and although it was completely useless, many a carpenter wouldn't buy a saw without it. When it finally was abandoned, two traditional blade forms remained: the straight-backed saw and the skew-backed saw. There is no difference whatever in performance, but the straight-backed form has the advantage of doubling as a straight edge for marking. Yet thousands of American craftsmen and almost all European and British craftsmen demand the skewbacked blade. Why? Sawmakers offer a simple answer: they're accustomed to it.

The chisel is the subject of assorted contradictions regarding its development and terminology. Many authorities, for example, venture the logical

The teeth of these ancient Egyptian saws were pointed backward to cut on the pull stroke, reducing the chance of buckling the soft metal blades of the time. Most Oriental saws are made this way today.

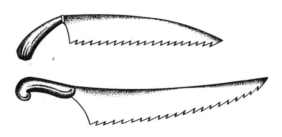

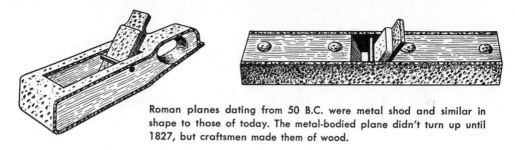

Roman planes dating from 50 B.C. were metal shod and similar in shape to those of today. The metal-bodied plane didn't turn up until 1827, but craftsmen made them of wood.

guess that the earliest metal chisels were made with a pointed tang like a file, as some still are. To forge a socket in which to fit the handle would appear too difficult with the crude tools of the remote past. Yet the oldest known examples of both types were found side by side at Bologna in a group of bronze tools 2,000 years old. As to the terminology, you have a choice of origins for the designation "firmer" chisel. Some claim it was originally called a "former" chisel because it formed the work before the paring chisel trimmed it. Others insist it's a firmer chisel because it's stronger, or firmer, than the paring type. When the two terms are combined to describe a common chisel type, they give rise to the age-old shop story of the apprentice who thought "socket firmer" meant hit it harder. (And you can.)

The plane has the most puzzling past of all the hand tools. The earliest museum examples, dating back twenty centuries, are all strangely modern in form. No truly primitive planes have ever been found. So it appears that the ancient Romans, who made most of the planes now in the museum displays, picked up their design fully developed. But where they picked it up is still a mystery. The same source may have furnished the design for boring bits found at their encampment sites. . . . bits so advanced they could be mistaken for at least one type in production today. As to the bit brace, it hasn't changed its basic form in the centuries since Egyptian art showed it in use building a mummy case.

Your hammer started out as a specially selected stone, called a hammer stone by archaeologists. Our Stone Age ancestors frequently chipped and ground a hollow in one side to provide a convenient thumb grip. Even the

Stone Age hammer (left) has no handle but is hollowed on one side for a comfortable thumb grip. When primitive man first put a handle on his hammer, he grooved the stone head (center) so a flexible withe could be bent around it and bound. Ancient Roman iron claw hammer (right), with broken claw, is remarkably modern in form.

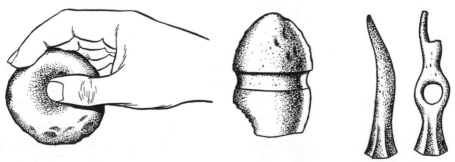

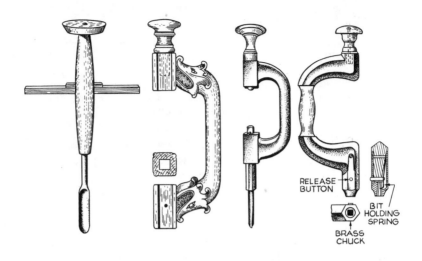

RELEASE BUTTON

BRASS CHUCK

BIT HOLDING SPRING

The bit brace of the early 19th century was often made by the man who used it, and handsomely carved to advertise his skill. Less elaborate models were sold to others.

Egyptian inventors of the mallet for chisel work used a simple hammer stone without a handle for everything else. And when the claw hammer came into being it was again the Romans who had it first. . . . in a form about halfway between today's ripping hammer and curved claw hammer.

The longer you work with tools and talk shop with others who do the more surprising facts you'll find, some with a touch of humor. You may already know your jack plane was originally called a jackass plane because it was the workhorse of its field.

But the tool story with the happiest ending got its start in South Shaftsbury, Vermont, at the end of the War of 1812. When the town's blacksmith, Silas Hawes, decided that metal carpenter's squares would be better than the usual wooden ones, he made a few from worn-out pit saw blades and stamped the scales on them by hand. The peddler who bought them found buyers so fast that Hawes had to give up blacksmithing and open a factory to fill the demand. With a patent on his squares and several more factories in his chain, blacksmith Hawes retired a few years later, independently wealthy. And his big steel squares, with a few tables added, are the framing squares of today . . . one of the most versatile tools in carpentry.

Sandpaper, our simplest tool, has a history with a climax that might well be an alchemist's dream. The story begins with the first record of a true abrasive, written in the Old Testament by the Hebrews. They referred to the sharpening of implements with a stone called Shamir, which, research indicates, is what we know today as emery. (It gets its present name from Cape Emeri on the Greek island of Naxos, where it has been mined for centuries.) But the first version of sandpaper seems to have been a thirteenth century

This center bit, found at an ancient Roman encampment, bears a striking resemblance to many high-speed power bits of today.

Chinese product, made by sticking crushed seashells to parchment with natural gums. The idea appears to have been lost from then until about 200 years ago when the Swiss revived it with crushed glass on paper backing. Although it worked it had a curious fault: the broken glass wasn't sharp enough. So flint, and later, crushed gems in the form of garnet, took its place. And a far more precious gem inspired the next step.

Searching for a way to make diamonds, early experimenters used a small electric furnace to cook a silica-carbon mix at close to 4,000 degrees. The result was described as "a few exceedingly sharp and hard crystals of a beautiful blue color." They were second only to the diamond in hardness but they were not diamonds. They were silicon carbide, the hardest and sharpest abrasive you can buy today. It costs more than ordinary sandpaper, but the price has come down a long way. Back in 1891, when those first beautiful blue crystals were produced, they cost as much as the diamonds they were supposed to imitate.

CHAPTER TWO

TOOLS FOR MEASURING AND MARKING

THERE ARE more than 3,000 different measuring and marking tools in regular use. Fortunately, you need only about a dozen for even very elaborate woodworking. And the average small shop does nicely with half that many or less, by using multipurpose tools that do the work of several. Seemingly minor features, too, can make an otherwise ordinary tool into a carpenter's favorite. Even the simple folding rule differs so much in detail that one type is often able to do a job another can't do.

The Boxwood Rule is the oldest of the folding rule family. Today, it's made mainly in 1' and 2' lengths. It holds its folded or extended position by the friction of its hinged joints. Extended, it has a smooth, flat surface to lay on the work—handy when a line must be drawn along it. It's available with numerals running from left to right (standard) or with numerals positioned parallel to the rule length, running in both directions. This double calibration makes it easy to take quick readings from either end in difficult locations, as in overhead work.

The Caliper Rule is a boxwood type (usually 1') with a built-in caliper. It quickly gauges the thickness of lumber or the diameter of round stock like a closet pole or dowel. Simply close the caliper against the stock to be measured and take the reading directly from the brass slide in thirty-secondths of an inch. It can also pinch hit as a marking guide for angle lines when the legs are set with a protractor.

The Zig-Zag Rule. This term is often applied to spring-joint folding rules in general (made by many manufacturers) but it is actually a trademark of Stanley Tools, the company that introduced it in the United States about 1899. The simplest form is about 7½" long folded, 6' long extended, with all section corners except the shorter end ones rounded to reduce wear on work clothes pockets.

The Extension Rule. This form has one end section that contains a calibrated slide-out brass extension for inside measurements, and all sections are square-ended to seat squarely against a surface. To take an inside measure-

Keep caliper rule folded to provide wide base in caliper operations. Jaws must reach to center of round stock.

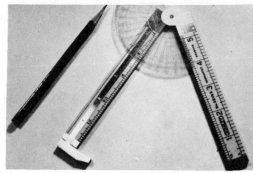

Use transparent protractor for angle marking. Radial center of protractor must be over rule's pivot pin.

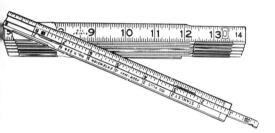

Zig-Zag extension rule has brass slide-out rule in one end section for making inside measurements.

Rule can be used as marking gauge in multiples of 2″. Here it marks 4″ width. Folded, end section marks at 2″ width.

ment, as between the sides of a doorway, unfold the rule just short of the doorway width starting with the extension rule end. Seat the partly folded end against one side of the doorway (all sections end exactly on an inch mark) and note the reading. Then pull out the extension at the other end and add its reading to the first one for the precise inside measurement. Standard rules are graduated in inches and sixteenths. Special models are made with feet divided into tenths and hundredths and with metric markings. The extension rule can also be used as a marking gauge. Use the Zig-Zag type where you need rigidity enough to reach across an opening like a wide doorway or stair well. For long spans with support only near one end hold the rule edge-up to prevent fishing pole flex, and avoid sudden whip-like movements that might cause breakage.

Steel Tape Rules, most compact of all types, are generally available in lengths from 6′ to 12′. For easy inside measuring, major manufacturers make the tape container exactly 2″ across the base. To take an inside measurement hold the container against one surface, extend the tape to the other, and add 2″ to the reading that shows where the tape emerges from the container. One Stanley rule makes it still easier by printing the inside measurements on the back of the tape with the 2″ already added.

An important feature of quality tape rules is the end hook, which always appears to be loosely rivetted. Actually, it is mounted to slide a distance

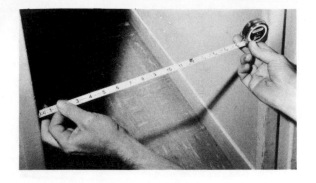

To take inside measurements with steel tape rule, extend it across opening and add 2″ to reading. *Rules courtesy of Stanley Tools.*

equal to its own thickness so both inside and outside measurements will be accurate. *Never* peen the rivets to tighten the hook. The average steel tape rule can be extended unsupported for a distance of about 3′. Where the tape is to be laid along a surface to permit marking at several points along the run a lock-button type is best. In locked position the tape is held extended and will not roll up automatically, so both your hands are left free. Release the button and the tape rolls back into the container.

Wing Dividers are used like a drawing compass to scribe circles and divide lines and arcs. But, unlike the compass, the divider has a quadrant-shaped "wing" running from one leg through a slot in the other. A knurled screw in the slotted leg is used to lock the quadrant in any set position, holding the points of the divider legs firmly so the gap between cannot change. (The compass setting is held only by friction in the pivot hinge.) In use, dividers are first set to the approximate spacing and screw-locked, as mentioned. The final precise setting is made with an adjusting screw in the other leg. Al-

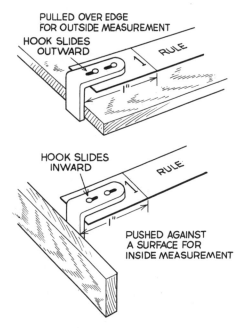

End hook of steel tape is mounted to slip a distance equal to its own thickness.

though the steel divider points offer maximum accuracy in marking, dividers that provide for replacing one point with a pencil are handier, as a pencil line or dot is much easier to follow than a pin prick or scratch. The difference in precision is too slight to be important in most woodworking.

Squares vary greatly in size, form, and purpose. Some are used only for marking and checking square cuts. Others also handle miters. Among the multipurpose squares are some of the most versatile tools made, with a range of uses from locating the center of a circle to figuring the amount of lumber in a house. The type of work you do determines the kind of square you need.

The *try square* has a short, thick handle joined to a longer thin metal blade at a 90-degree angle. It gets its name from its use in "trying" or testing the squareness of corners. But you'll use it most for drawing lines for squared saw cuts. In testing squareness, the handle is held firmly against one surface and the blade brought into contact with the other. The appearance of light between blade edge and wood surface indicates which areas are off square. Dark areas are planed or sanded to close the gap. The square can also be used as a marking gauge if you develop the knack of holding a pencil fixed against the blade edge while sliding the handle along a board edge.

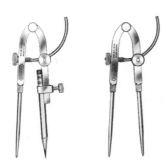

Wing dividers are made with point on each leg (right) and with one leg point interchangeable with pencil (left). Latter type is more versatile.

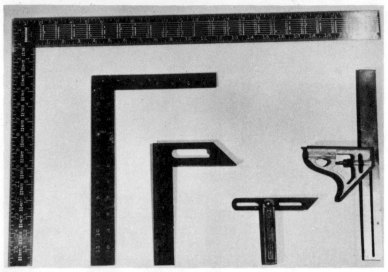

Common squares and related tools (left to right): framing square for calculating and marking; 1-foot square for measuring and marking; try square for checking and marking; sliding T-bevel for marking and checking angles; combination square for multiple use.

When using try square to mark line for cutting, hold handle firmly against the board edge and use pencil to scribe along blade.

To use try square as marking gauge, hold pencil point at blade, slide handle along board edge.

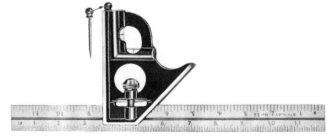

Combination square has levels set in handle at right angles to each other. Pointed scriber for marking is also housed in handle, held by threaded, knurled cap.

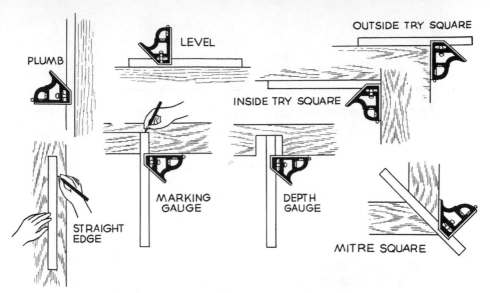

Eight different uses of the combination square. *Courtesy Stanley Tools.*

Combination "set" has combination-square handle plus a protractor head that can be set at any angle, and centering head (right) for finding the center of round stock.

The *try and miter square* is a try square with the blade end of the handle cut at 45 degrees. Hold this edge against a board edge and the blade crosses the board at 45 degrees for marking a miter.

The *combination square* is more than half a dozen valuable tools in one. It serves as a try square, miter gauge, marking gauge, depth gauge, level and plumb, straightedge, and foot rule. The handle, with an angle of 90 degrees on one edge, 45 on the other, can be clamped at any point along the blade. It can also be reversed in position or removed completely. Quality models have at least one spirit level and a scriber for marking. Clamp the blade tip at any desired distance from the handle edge, hold a pencil point against it, and you have a marking gauge. Set the handle edge on the wood surface and slip the blade down into a mortise and the ruled edge tells you the depth. Use the handle alone, as a level, or set the blade against a vertical surface with the handle in place and use the level glass to check plumbness.

The *combination set* is a combination square plus a centering head, to

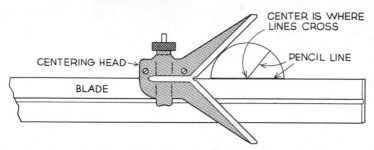

CENTER IS WHERE LINES CROSS

CENTERING HEAD →

PENCIL LINE

BLADE

To find center of round stock with centering head, hold stock against V edges of head with blade across end of stock. Draw a line across end of stock along blade edge that emerges from V center. Then give stock about a quarter turn and draw another line. Where the lines cross you have the exact center.

To set sliding T-bevel with protractor place bevel on top of protractor with pivot nut loosened. Then swing blade to desired angle and tighten wing-nut.

When a bevel is being planed by hand, set the T-bevel to the desired angle and use it in try-square fashion to check accuracy as work progresses.

locate the center of round stock and a protractor head to permit setting the blade at any required angle. It does all the jobs of the combination square and quite a few more.

The *sliding T bevel* is like a try square with a blade adjustable to any angle. The slotted blade can be extended to either side of the handle or centered to form the T that accounts for the name. It can be set to any angle with the aid of a protractor or it may be adjusted to an existing bevel or angle cut so others can be made to match. Once in position it is locked by a clamp screw. It can be used to mark for beveling and to check the accuracy of a bevel being planed.

The *framing square* is not only a marking square but a one-piece calculating machine. It enables you to determine in seconds rafter lengths for various roof pitches, the angle cuts at rafter ends, stair stringer layout, the board footage of various pieces of lumber and many other essential factors in woodworking and carpentry. You find and use the calibrations that do these jobs according to their location on the following parts of the square.

The *body,* or blade, of the square is the longer and wider leg, usually 24″ by 2″.

The *tongue* is shorter and narrower, usually 16″ by 1½″.

The *heel* is the outside corner where body and tongue meet.

The *face* is the side on which the manufacturer's name is stamped. (The one shown is a Stanley.)

The *back* is the side opposite the face.

As the angle calculations are based on roof structures (though they apply also to such things as stairways), you'll be using the following basic roof terms when you work with the square.

The *span* is the distance between the outside edges of the supporting wall plates, the horizontal members that cap the wall.

The *unit of span* is a framing square term and is always 24″.

The *rise* is the *vertical* distance from the plate height to the ridge, or peak, of the roof.

The *run* is the *horizontal* distance from the ridge to the outer edge of the plate. In the equally pitched roof this is simply half the span.

The *pitch* is the amount of slope from the ridge down to the plate.

Pitch can be expressed in two different ways. For one, it can be the ratio of the *rise* to the *span*. This way, if you have an 8′ rise and a 24′ span you divide 24 into 8 and get a ratio of ⅓, which is called ⅓ pitch. If the rise was 6′ with a 24′ span you'd have a ¼ pitch.

The other method of expressing pitch is in inches of vertical *rise per foot of run*. This is the figure you need for the framing square and it's almost magically easy to get it even if all you know is the pitch ratio—⅓, for example. Simply multiply it by the *unit of span*, which is 24″. One third times 24″ gives you 8″, your rise in inches per foot of run. The same system works on any other ratio. The rest is just as easy.

To Find Rafter Length, hold the square face up, body at the top, heel to your right. At the left end of the body you'll see the words "Length of Common Rafters Per Foot of Run" at the top of a list that includes all regular rafter types. Now simply look along the inch markings on the outer edge of

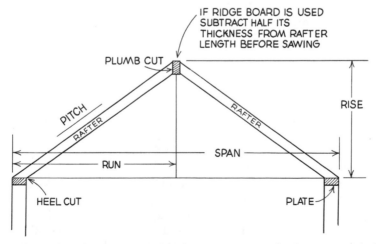

These are the roof framing terms used in framing-square work. They are applied to any other angular structure to be laid out with the square.

23	22	21	20	19	18	17
LENGTH	COMMON	RAFTERS	PER FOOT	RUN	21 63	20 81
"	HIP OR	VALLEY	"	"	24 74	24 02
DIFF	IN LENGTH	OF JACKS	16 INCHES	CENTERS	28 7/8	27 3/4
"	"	"	2 FEET	"	43 1/4	41 5/8
SIDE	CUT	OF	JACKS	USE	6 11/16	6 15/16
"	"	HIP OR	VALLEY	"	8 1/4	8 1/2

Pencil points to line on which common rafter lengths are calculated. Other standard rafters are listed on lines below it.

12	11	10	9	8	7	6
16 97	16 28	15 62	15	14 42	13 89	13 42
20 78	20 22	19 70	19 21	18 76	18 36	18
22 5/8	21 11/16	20 13/16	20	19 1/4	18 1/2	17 7/8
33 15/16	32 9/16	31 1/4	30	28 7/8	27 3/4	26 13/16
8 1/2	8 7/8	9 1/4	9 5/8	10	10 3/8	10 3/4
9 7/8	10 1/8	10 3/8	10 5/8	10 7/8	11 1/16	11 5/8

Pencil points to 8″ mark along upper body edge, indicating 8″ rise per foot of run. On top line in column under 8 are figures 14-42, the number of inches and decimals per foot run. Multiply the total run in feet by this figure to get rafter length.

the body until you come to 8″—your rise per foot of run. In the first line directly under it you'll find the figures 14.42, the number of inches and decimals of common rafter length for each foot of run. If you're using the 24′ *span* given in the earlier example, the run of an equally pitched roof will be half of it, or 12′. Multiply 12 by 14.42 and you get 173.04—the length in inches of the rafter required. Use the nearest tenth for practical purposes. (On the back of the square the inner edge of the tongue is marked in inches and tenths). If a ridge board is used between the rafters where they meet at the ridge (usually the case) subtract half its thickness from the rafter length before cutting.

To draw the cutting angle lines at the ends of the rafter first mark it to the length calculated by the square. To mark the cut at the ridge (called the plumb cut) lay the square on the rafter, heel downward, tongue to the right. (The major rafter length should be to your left.) Set the 8″ mark on the outer edge of the tongue directly on the upper edge of the rafter. (This represents the 8″ rise.) Swing the blade to bring the 12″ mark on its outer edge directly on the rafter's upper edge. With the square in this position, slide it until the outer edge of the tongue crosses the measure line's length mark. Draw a line along this edge of the tongue at this point and you have your sawing line.

Set the square in the same position for the "heel" cut at the lower end, but slide it so the outer edge of the *blade,* not the tongue, crosses the measure line's length mark. Draw a line along that edge at that point and you have your sawing line.

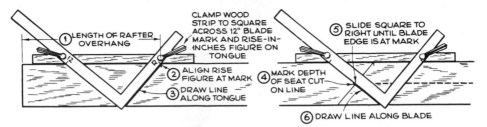

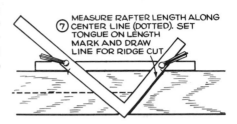

One way of measuring and marking rafter: Start from length of overhang. Mark notch for seat cut. Measure rafter length from outer corner of notch along measure line (dotted) and mark opposite end. Then set square against mark and draw line for·ridge cut.

The Wood Marking Gauge is used to mark for a saw cut parallel to the edge of a board or panel. It's a short, thick wooden rule fitted through a sliding block that can be clamped by a thumbscrew at any point along it. A pin projecting downward from the rule tip does the marking by making a scratch. Slide the rule out so the pin rests at the width cut desired, clamp it, and slide the block along the board edge with light pressure on the pin. It's a simple and efficient tool, though some users prefer a pencil line to a scratch. For these, one of the methods described previously for marking-gauge work with a rule or square is a better answer.

The Butt Gauge is used to mark recesses for butt hinges so the surface of the hinge leaf will be flush with the surface of the wood. Though smaller, it operates much like a wood marking gauge. It uses a pointed "cutter" to mark the rectangular outline of the recess to be made, and the depth to which it is to be cut. To use it, set the marking cutter bar so the cutter will scribe the hinge width on door and jamb, allowing for the usual setback. The squared flange on the marking gauge permits its use as a try square for marking the end lines of the hinge recesses.

Wood marking gauges vary in detail. Angular cross section of rule in this Stanley gauge holds marking pin at angle for marking without digging in. To mark in either direction, gauge rule is tilted so pin always angles backward.

Butt gauge is miniature metal marking gauge. Ends are square with base to serve as marking square. Cutter bar is adjusted to mark hinge leaf width, then thickness. Ends of leaf outline are marked by using gauge as a square.

CHAPTER THREE

SAWS

THE RIGHT SAW for the job makes the going easy. With a sharp ripsaw you can run through a 1" thick pine board at about 10' a minute, using normal, easy strokes. A good crosscut saw can work just as fast across the grain. So sawing should not be an unwelcome chore. If it is, the trouble is either in the saw or in your choice of a saw unsuited to the job. In either event there's always a remedy.

To handle all the everyday woodworking cuts you need five different saw types—six if you include a hacksaw for the occasional metal cutting most woodworkers find necessary. An understanding of seemingly unimportant details of these saws and how to use them properly can make a major difference in the time and effort required in cutting. The number of teeth per inch is an example. The fewer the teeth in a woodsaw (within the normal range) the faster and rougher the cut. More teeth mean a slower, smoother-surfaced cut. In a hacksaw the number of teeth per inch must be matched to the type and thickness of the material to be cut, as listed later. A bad choice can slow the cutting greatly, in some cases break the teeth.

In each saw, basic design factors, often too small to notice, determine its suitability for a specific job. When you know what to look for it's easy to spot the details that count.

The Crosscut Saw is designed to cut across the grain, as in cutting a board to length. In its most popular form it has a blade 26" long. Smaller ones of 22", 20", and 12" are made to fit toolboxes, and are slightly slower working. Quality is important in a crosscut saw. The teeth of better grades are beveled on both edges to form miniature knife points. On lower-quality models they are not. They have the outline of crosscut teeth but the square edges of ripsaw teeth. Result: slower cutting with greater effort. This may not be important for occasional use, but it is very important in extensive work.

In all grades alternate teeth are "set," or bent, outward to opposite sides to make a cut wider than the blade thickness so the saw can move freely. (The teeth actually make two parallel cuts at once, crumbling out the inter-

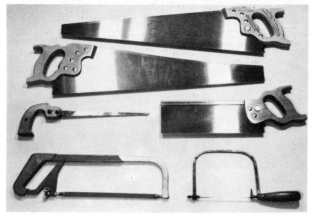

Common workshop saws. Top to bottom: straight-back ripsaw; skew-back crosscut; left, compass saw; right, backsaw; left, hacksaw; right, coping saw.

A taper-ground crosscut saw.

vening wood as the saw moves.) If you expect to cut damp, green, or pitchy wood, the *taper ground* blade is an additional feature that eases sawing. This blade form, used on the Disston saws shown in the photos, is actually thinner at the back edge than at the toothed edge. It is also thinner at the tip than at the butt, or handle end. The extra blade clearance lets it cut easily in wet wood that would jam an ordinary saw.

Smoothness and speed of cutting depends on the number of teeth per inch, or "points." The fewer teeth, the faster the cut; the more teeth, the smoother. Crosscut saws commonly run the range of eight, ten, and twelve points. If you also have a backsaw (described shortly), favor a coarse-toothed crosscut for speed, and use the backsaw where smoothness is important. Both the backsaw and miter-box type are made fine-toothed only.

Cutting is fastest when the angle between the cutting edge of the saw and the wood surface is 45 degrees. But any angle, even vertical or parallel to the surface, will work, though more slowly. Start the cut at the butt of the blade with slow draw strokes, then continue with full strokes. If the saw veers away from the pencil line, as in cutting across a wide plywood panel, flex it *slightly* toward the line as you saw and it will return to it. Don't flex it much or it may "over-steer" and veer across to the other side. (Too much flex can also cause the saw to jam or possibly buckle, causing permanent damage.)

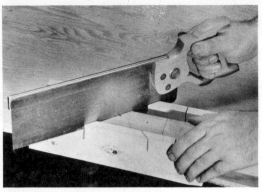

How to steer a saw: If cut starts to veer off line, flex saw slightly to lead it back.

Backsaw has stiffener along back of blade to prevent flexing, assure straight cut. Use it in miter-box work.

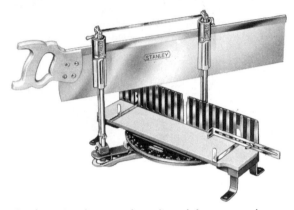

Stanley miter box can be adjusted for any angle cut, holds saw horizontal as cut progresses.

Always use a crosscut saw on plywood regardless of the direction of the surface grain. It cuts with minimum fraying of outer veneers. Favor a crosscut also, when a single saw must be chosen for field work. It is used more often than the ripsaw on most jobs. If you lack a miter-box saw the crosscut is your best pinch hitter. Take slow strokes to avoid saw tip whip.

The Ripsaw is designed to cut parallel to the wood grain, to saw a board lengthwise. The leading edges of its teeth are more nearly perpendicular to the cutting edge, and there is no bevel. In operation the teeth act as tiny chisels. (Slide the teeth of a sharp ripsaw flat along the surface of a piece of wood with the grain and you'll see they actually make minute shavings instead of sawdust.) As on crosscut saws, the teeth are set to provide blade clearance, and taper-ground blades are available. The usual blade length is 26″. All are coarser-toothed than crosscuts, typically about five and a half point (five and a half teeth per inch). At the tip of the blade, however, a good ripsaw is one tooth finer (six and a half points) so cutting is started with the tip of the blade rather than the butt, as with the crosscut. The angle between the cutting edge and the wood surface should be about 60 degrees for easy working on boards of average thickness, 45 degrees on thin boards like clapboards.

Compass saw is used to make curved or straight cuts too far from panel edge for frame of coping saw.

Important application of compass saw is starting straight cut from hole bored in panel. It can make entire cut, or make starting cut for larger saw.

In all sawing (crosscutting and ripping) use as much of the blade length as possible so as not to concentrate wear at the midsection. Take easy, natural strokes. Forcing the saw with rapid strokes adds little to speed and sacrifices accuracy.

The Backsaw is a rectangular blade with a metal reinforcing strip along the back edge to prevent flexing. Length ranges from 10″ to 16″. In 26″ to 28″ length it is called a *miter-box saw*. Both are fine-toothed (in crosscut pattern) ranging from eleven point to thirteen point, and are used mainly in miter boxes to make cuts for joints and miters. They are not tipped downward in cutting, like rip or crosscut types, but are kept parallel to the surface throughout the cut. Keeping the saw level while cutting in a simple wooden miter box is especially important when making such joints as half laps (where wood is cut only half way through) as the depth must be the same at both ends of the cut. Some factory-made, adjustable miter boxes keep the saw level automatically.

The Dovetail Saw is the smallest of the backsaw types, ranging in blade length from about 8″ to 12″. It is designed for extremely fine joint work and in typical form has a fifteen point blade. To get the utmost cutting precision, score the line to be cut with a sharp-pointed knife three or four times. Use the knife to peel away some of the wood on the waste side of the line—the side on which more wood will be removed to form the joint recess. Then place the saw flush against the remaining straight side of the knife cut, and make the saw cut.

The Compass Saw has a narrow, tapered blade, usually less than 1″ wide at the butt, pointed at the tip, and 12″ to 14″ in length. It is used to make both curved and straight cuts, but must be used perpendicular to the surface for curved work. It cannot cut on as small a radius as the coping saw but cuts faster and is better suited to working in thick stock. It can start from a hole in a panel area too far from the edge for the frame reach of a coping saw. When a straight cut is to be started from a hole bored through a panel the compass saw makes the initial cut long enough for a larger saw to be inserted. The larger saw, such as a crosscut, finishes the cut faster. For average curve cutting you can use the entire length of the blade. For small radius work use the narrower section near the tip.

Saw knife with interchangeable blades used as compass
saw for cutting wallboard.

Coping saw is used for fine, ornate cutting. Blade can be
pivoted to face in any direction so frame can reach over
edge. Work should be clamped firmly to bench.

The Keyhole Saw, often confused with the compass saw, has a narrower
blade, usually 10″ to 12″ long. As its name implies, it was once actually used
for cutting keyholes. This is the saw for tight radius cutting in areas that
cannot be reached by a coping saw. In working with the compass and keyhole saws, keep your eye on the saw to avoid any flexing. The narrow blades
bend easily, but can usually be straightened by hand or with pliers.

The Coping Saw is a small frame saw with a very narrow blade held taut
between the frame ends. It is used to make smooth, accurate, curved cuts,
as in fitting wood against a molding, and to cut very small radius curves in
ornamental scroll work. Inexpensive, replaceable blades are available, in
widths of ⅛″ and less, for cutting both wood and metal. The blade may be
revolved in the frame by turning the end fittings, so the cutting edge may
face downward, upward, or at any angle between. This allows the frame to
be swung over the nearest wood edge without changing the cutting direction.
The blades are mounted with the teeth pointing toward the handle, to cut
on the pull stroke. If pointed the other way the drag of the cutting stroke
would spring the frame end inward, slackening the blade and inviting frequent breakage. You hold the saw with one hand, never with two, like a
hacksaw. For extensive work, a saddle like that shown in the drawing is
handy, as the work may be shifted or turned as necessary.

The Hacksaw has a rigid frame to permit adequate tension on the blade
with no chance of blade-slackening "spring." The blade is mounted with
teeth pointing forward to cut on the push stroke. In use, you hold the saw
with your right hand on the handle, your left on the front corner of the frame.
Apply moderate downward pressure with both hands on the forward stroke,
then ease off on the return stroke.

Selecting a blade with the correct number of teeth per inch for the material is very important. In general, use fine teeth on thin stock, coarse teeth
on thick stock. The coarse ones cut faster, the fine ones slower, but with less
chance of breakage. For average work the blades are made of standard high-
speed steel.

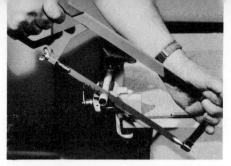

Hold hacksaw like this, applying moderate pressure at both ends during forward stroke. Release pressure on back stroke.

Saddle made from scrap wood and clamped in vise is handy for supporting coping-saw work.

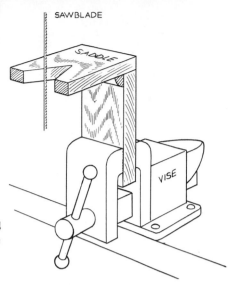

Where maximum wearing quality is needed a molybdenum alloy is used, and for extremely tough material cutting, a tungsten alloy. The type of alloy is usually printed on the blade. All types are made in four different tooth spacings, for use as follows:

Teeth per inch	
14	soft solid steel, iron, brass, bronze, copper, and aluminum.
18	tool steel, iron pipe, light angle iron, general shop work.
24	drill rod, medium sheet metal, tubing. Best tooth size for hard materials.
32	thin sheet metal, thin-walled tubing, and stock less than .085" thick.

Where the work is too thin for at least two teeth to rest on the edge being cut, tip the stock at an angle that provides enough surface for two or more teeth. If a blade breaks when cutting thicker stock, do not start a new blade in the same cut. The unworn teeth will be wider than the cut and will jam

Hacksaw teeth with regular set have one tooth set to left, then one without set (called a raker) followed by one set to right. This type is used to cut material of uniform size, and for contour cutting.

Wavy set hacksaw teeth are set in groups, or waves, to reduce strain on individual teeth. This is a good type of blade to use on thin stock.

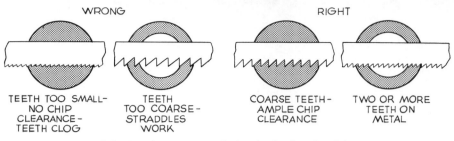

WRONG   RIGHT

TEETH TOO SMALL– NO CHIP CLEARANCE – TEETH CLOG

TEETH TOO COARSE – STRADDLES WORK

COARSE TEETH – AMPLE CHIP CLEARANCE

TWO OR MORE TEETH ON METAL

Selecting the proper tooth size for hacksawing jobs.

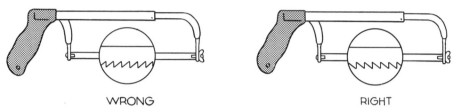

WRONG   RIGHT

Hacksaw teeth should face forward, not backward like coping-saw teeth.

and possibly break in it. Turn the work over and start a new cut from the other side to meet the first one.

Care and Sharpening of Wood Saws. To reduce the frequency of sharpening, take a careful look at the teeth of your saw when they are new. A magnifying glass will help. Touch up the teeth from time to time with a file of the size listed at the end of the chapter for the saw's point count. Simply sharpen the tooth edges, keeping the same shape.

If the saw is worn dull, the first sharpening step is called "jointing." This brings all teeth to an even height. (Short teeth don't cut, high teeth dig in and cause jumping or buckling.) To joint a saw rest a mill file (with handle removed) lengthwise along the teeth. Slide the file back and forth until it touches the top of all teeth. The high teeth will have small flat spots on the tips at this stage.

Shape the teeth next by using the proper file, as listed, and filing at right angles across the saw. The saw should be held in a filing clamp or between wood blocks held firmly in a vise. The top of the clamp should be no more than ⅛″ below the saw tooth gullets to prevent file-dulling "chatter." Do no beveling at this time. If you are not sure of the correct tooth shape, look at the unworn teeth almost always found at the butt of the blade. In reshaping a high tooth, file from one edge until you reach the midpoint of the flat area caused by jointing. Then file from the other edge until the tooth is again pointed. Even when there is no irregularity in the height of a dull saw's teeth, a *light* jointing is helpful. Making a very small, flat spot on the tooth tips serves as a guide in filing.

Setting the teeth is not necessary every time a saw is given a light sharpening. This is the process of bending alternate teeth to left and right. If the saw is worn enough to require setting it should be done with a "saw set" made for the purpose, as no more than the upper half of each tooth should

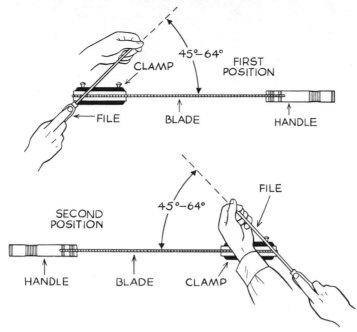

How crosscut-saw teeth are beveled. Use file size to match number of teeth per inch. (See listing.) Angle is not critical within range shown, but all teeth must have the same bevel.

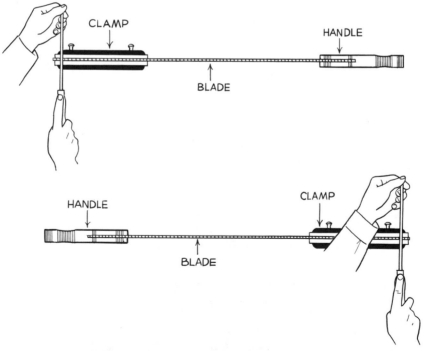

Ripsaw teeth are simply filed straight across. Two positions are used because of set. Move saw so clamp is always under filing area.

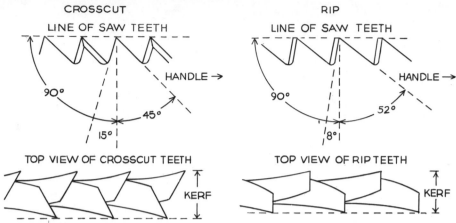

Difference between shape of ripsaw teeth and crosscut. Both are set to provide cut (kerf) wider than thickness of saw blade.

be bent. Deeper setting can crimp or crack the blade, even break the tooth.

Final filing is begun with the saw clamped in front of you, teeth up, *handle to the right.* Start at the tip of the saw. Pick the first tooth set *toward* you and place the file in the gullet to the *left* of it. Skip the next gullet to the right and file in the following one, repeating the process until you reach the butt of the blade. You will always be filing in a gullet to the left of a tooth set toward you. Now reverse the saw in the clamp, placing the handle to the left. Start at the saw tip again, pick the first tooth set toward you and place the file in the gullet to the *right* of it. Take a close look and you'll see this is the first of the gullets you skipped when you filed the other side of the saw. Now skip the next gullet and file the following one, as before, until you reach the end of the blade.

On a ripsaw do all this filing at right angles to the blade to make squared edges on the teeth. On a crosscut saw hold the file handle to the left during the first stage of filing when the saw handle is to the right. It then bevels the back of the tooth to the left and the front of the tooth to the right at the same time. The bevel angle can be between 45 and 64 degrees, but all teeth should be filed at the same angle. After the first side of the blade is filed, skipping every other gullet, as described for shaping teeth, reverse the saw in the clamp so the handle is to the left, and repeat the procedure, this time holding the file handle to the right. Although the idea suggests itself, do not attempt to file both bevels from the same side of the saw. Experience shows they will then vary enough to make the saw run or veer to one side or the other in use.

Table of File Sizes for Saw Sharpening

4½, 5½, 6 points—7 inch Slim Taper.
7, 8 points—6 inch Slim Taper.
11, 12, 13, 14, 15 points—4½ inch Slim Taper.
Over 16 points—5 inch Superfine Metal Saw File, No. 2 Cut.
Jointing teeth—8 or 10 inch Mill Bastard.

CHAPTER FOUR

CHISELS

MATCHING A CHISEL to a job today is much easier than in the past, as each type can handle a wider range of work. Modern alloy blades need not be as thick to be strong, so they can perform delicate as well as heavy-duty operations. And the tang chisel, once relatively fragile because the wooden handle was often split by the tang on which it was mounted, now has a plastic handle that makes it as tough as the socket chisel. The most rugged of all wood chisels has a metal-cored plastic handle. Inside it, the blade shank meets the shank of a steel cap mounted on the handle head so impact force is transmitted entirely by metal, from cap to cutting edge. Like the heavy-duty, plastic-handled tang chisels, it can be driven by any type of hammer. The old rule, "never drive a chisel with anything but a wooden mallet," doesn't apply. So you have a wide choice in chisel construction.

Size is a basic factor in selecting a chisel. *The butt chisel* is the shortest, with a blade 2½″ to 3¼″ long, and an overall length from around 7¾″ to 9″, in widths from ¼″ to 2″. This is the type for work in limited space. *The pocket chisel,* now the most popular size, is larger, with a blade length of 4″ to 5″, overall length from about 9″ to 10¼″. This is the handiest size for general use. Widths usually run from ¼″ to 2″. The *mill chisel* is the largest, with a blade length of 8″ to 10″ and an overall length of around 16″ or more. Widths are usually in the 1″ to 2″ range. This one isn't likely to figure in average shop work.

The purpose for which the chisel is designed is the other factor in its choice. One type, the framing, or mortising chisel, was originally used in the heavy-duty mortising of building framework, a practice that vanished with modern construction methods. So you're not likely to have much need for the tool, nor much chance of finding one easily. The other two classifications are important, however.

The Paring Chisel has a thin blade traditionally ground to a 15-degree cutting bevel. It is driven by hand only, for light shave cuts, as in joint fitting. Today the factory-ground cutting edge is usually beveled around 25 degrees.

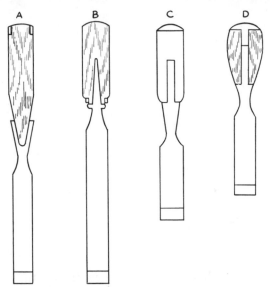

Basic chisel construction: A. Traditional socket chisel with wooden handle fitted to blade socket. B. Traditional wooden-handled tang chisel. C. Modern plastic-handled tang chisel. D. Metal-core handled chisel.

What they look like (from left): wood-handled, leather-capped butt chisel; wood-handled, leather-capped firmer chisel; plastic-handled tang chisel for paring work; heavy-duty tang chisel with plastic handle and metal cap, for hammer-driving.

Reground to 15 degrees, it cuts more easily but the thinner edge is more prone to chipping.

The Firmer Chisel has a thicker blade than the paring chisel and was originally ground to about a 20-degree cutting-edge bevel. It was designed to be driven by hand or mallet in medium-duty work such as light mortising. Today, with metal-capped plastic handle, it is suited to both medium

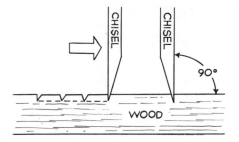

End cut of recess or mortise is always made with bevel facing other end of recess (right), so flat side of blade makes straight downward entry. Make cut across both ends, then a series of notch cuts between. In notching, keep bevel facing direction of progress (left).

Notching mortise cut with metal-core-handled chisel to clean out recess.

and heavy duty. The common factory-ground bevel is around 25 degrees, the same as the traditional bevel of the framing and mortising chisels it largely replaces.

The Gouge is a chisel with a hollow-shaped blade. It's a specialized tool for cutting rounded grooves.

How to Use a Chisel. In general don't use a chisel for work another tool can do better. A chisel can trim the edge of a board, for example, but a plane can do it better. The most important use of the chisel is in forming recesses and mortises, though in the latter it should usually play a secondary role after an auger bit has bored out most of the material.

To make a shallow recess, as for a hinge leaf, start by drawing the outline of the recess on the wood surface. Then, with sharp-pointed knife score the lines that run parallel with the grain. This prevents splitting out of the surface fibers during the chisel work. Next, set the chisel at one end of the outline with its edge on the across-grain line, bevel facing the other end, and strike the head with a wooden mallet or hammer. Never hammer-drive a chisel with the cutting edge parallel to the grain, as splitting is certain to result. Only paring cuts can be made safely in this direction. (If you're a beginner, try driving the chisel in scrap wood first to gauge the force so you

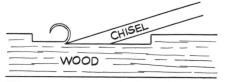

If recess extends to edge of wood, as in hinge work, remove loosened stock by paring inward from edge with bevel up.

Where recess is completely enclosed remove stock from one end toward the other with bevel down. Make cut in uphill direction of grain.

Partially cleared recess with short section cleared at left. Narrow sections between chisel cuts have already been loosened by bevel's wedging action, making removal easy.

won't cut too deep.) Repeat the process at the other mortise end. Then make a series of cuts about ⅛″ apart parallel to the end cut, working toward the other end. The bevel of the blade should face in the direction of progress. Its wedging action tends to loosen the narrow intervening sections. If the recess extends to an edge of the wood, as in hinge work, the chisel-notched material is easily removed by first paring inward from the corner, then downward from the notched surface. If the recess does not extend to an edge (a completely enclosed outline) work from one end toward the other, guiding the chisel with the left hand, pushing it with the right. In this, a bevel-down blade position gives the best control of paring action. As the sections are somewhat pre-loosened by wedging action, they come out easily.

Mortises should be made by first boring out most of the material inside the outline with a series of slightly overlapping auger bit holes. The chisel is then used for paring cuts to shave away the projecting points of material remaining between holes, and to trim the sides flat. At the corners work the chisel cross grain first, into the rounded portion. In the early stages the wood will usually crumble out. Near the corner it may be necessary to follow each cross grain cut with a paring cut parallel to the grain. Always cut across the grain first to provide a definite limit for the paring cut so there's no chance of with-the-grain splitting beyond the mortise.

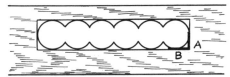

Deep mortise made by series of overlapping holes, remaining material pared out with chisel. At corners always make cross cut (A) before with-the-grain cut (B).

Hold the paring chisel like this to shave off stock between bored holes. Take light cuts, moving chisel downward with blade edge tipped to an angle. Rock chisel from side to side to aid cutting in stubborn wood.

Partially completed mortise looks like this. Right end has been squared, also lower left corner. In pine, entire job was completed in about four minutes.

Paring across the grain, as in smoothing the bottom of a half-lap joint, is done in stages. Pare inward and slightly upward from one side toward the center, then from the other side in the same manner. This prevents splitting out the edges, as the blade does not pass outward over them. The slight mound of material remaining in the center is then removed with horizontal paring cuts from each side.

Chamfering and trimming are sometimes done with the chisel, especially in repair or remodeling work where the location does not permit the use of another tool, such as a plane. Always move the chisel in the direction of the "uphill" grain so it won't dig in. Guide it with the left hand gripping the blade and push it with the right. Use it bevel down for roughing, bevel up and flat on the wood for paring.

Sharpening a Chisel. Whetting a chisel occasionally on an oilstone keeps a keen edge on it with a minimum of re-grinding. If the cutting edge bevel is the usual 25 to 30 degrees, whet it at a slightly steeper angle, say 30 to 35 degrees. This way you whet the cutting edge only rather than the entire bevel, greatly speeding the job because far less metal is involved in producing the edge. Keep the stone moist with oil so metal particles won't clog its pores. Seat the bevel firmly on the stone, then tip the chisel handle very slightly higher. Move the blade back and forth in steady position over the stone. Don't let the handle rock up and down or you'll round the cutting edge. You can tell when the blade is sharp by feeling it carefully. Then turn

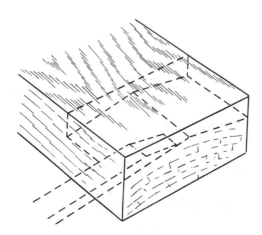

When leveling surface that runs through stock from edge to edge, as in lap joints, work from one edge to the center, with chisel aimed slightly upward. Repeat process from other side. Then level off central hump with paring cuts.

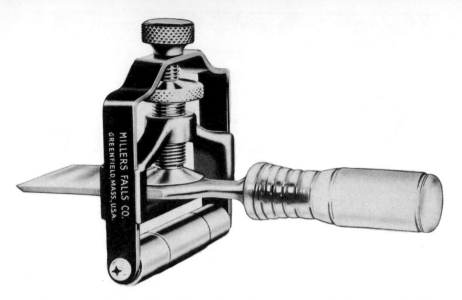

Chisel sharpener made by Millers Falls holds chisel at pre-set angle. Roller permits it to be moved back and forth over whetstone without danger of rocking.

it over, lay the flat side on the stone and slide it back and forth a few times to remove the "wire" or feather edge turned over by whetting the bevel. If any small nicks show up at this time (revealed by shiny spots on the edge) repeat both whetting steps. When the edge is smooth and keen give it a final touch with a few strokes on a razor strop. Experts make a final test by dry-shaving the hair on the back of the wrist with the chisel edge. It should cut without pulling.

The chisel sharpener is a very handy tool for whetting, as it makes the job easy and foolproof, and most types can also be used on plane irons. The device is simply a clamp with a roller on it. Tighten it on the chisel blade, adjusted to the desired whetting angle, and move the cutting edge back and forth over the stone with the roller supporting the other end and maintaining the set angle. There is no chance of off-angle honing or rounding.

Grinding a chisel is a simple job on the power grinder. It is necessary when the edge is nicked or worn down by many whettings. The blade, supported by the grinding wheel rest, is held against the upper portion of the wheel and moved in a straight line across it from side to side. It must be kept square with the wheel axis to assure a square cutting edge. The curve of the wheel perimeter produces a slightly hollow grind. This is the best type of cutting edge for a chisel if the wheel is of average size. Very small wheels produce too deep a hollow and a thin, fragile edge. To get the 25- to 30-degree bevel, make the beveled surface slightly longer than twice the thickness of the blade at the bevel area.

For very precise model work some woodworkers grind their chisels to a bevel of 15 degrees or less. As a hollow grind of this slim section would be impracticably fragile, they use a flat bevel. To produce it they work against the flat surface of a sanding plate, using aluminum-oxide cloth bonded on as the abrasive.

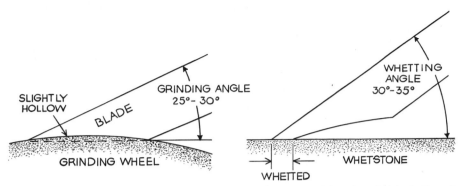

Difference between grinding angle and whetting angle. Ground bevel is slightly hollowed by grinding wheel. Whetted bevel is flat, as is surface of whetstone.

A badly damaged blade with deep nicks or chips should have the damaged portion of the edge removed before re-grinding. This is done by setting the grinder's tool rest slightly below the center of the wheel and moving the chisel edge into the wheel on a radius line, that is, pointed directly at the hub of the wheel. It is moved from side to side just as in regrinding, until all nicks and chips are ground away. Then the tool rest is re-set so the bevel can be ground on the upper portion of the wheel. In all grinding work it is important to dip the blade tip in water frequently to prevent damage from overheating. Keep a jar of water close to the grinder for this purpose, as the thin blade section heats rapidly.

CHAPTER FIVE

PLANES

THE PLANE is one of the easiest woodworking tools to use. For smoothing or shaving stock, all you need do is push it along the wood surface to pare off shavings until the job is done. It can't split the wood as a chisel might in the same operation, as the narrow slit—called the mouth—through which the shavings pass will not admit a heavy slice. Also, if a thicker layer of wood

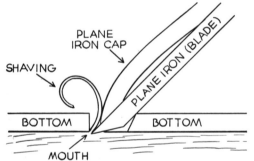

Why a plane can't split wood. Shaving is bent sharply upward by angle of plane iron. If thick slice of wood starts to lift it is sheared off, as heavy layer can't pass through plane's mouth.

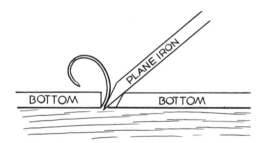

Block plane and modelmaker's plane have plane iron mounted bevel up to shave through end grain.

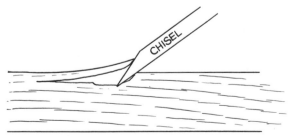

A chisel, without plane's narrow mouth, would lift thick layer of wood in irregular grain areas and cause splitting.

starts to lift at irregular grain areas, the steep blade angle breaks it off against the front edge of the mouth, only a fraction of an inch from the cutting edge. The blade—called the plane iron—then shears off the broken end. This is the cause of the pitted surface that sometimes results from planing irregular grain. Even this can be avoided by adjusting the plane for a hair-thin shaving.

A few basic rules eliminate most planing troubles before they occur. For a first step, always examine the wood and always plane in the "uphill" direction of the grain, as shown in the photo. If you plane in the downhill direction you will snag the grain ends and roughen the surface. On any work, don't let the plane sag over the ends of the wood at the start and finish of the stroke. This rounds the corners. Instead, hold the bottom of the plane snug against the surface being planed so the plane is always level, even and flat. If you are planing end grain (like the end of a board) plane inward from one edge to the center, then from the other edge, so the blade never passes over the far edge. If it does it will split the edge. The high spot that remains in the center of the board end is planed off last. Another end-grain method, shown in the photo, calls for scrap wood clamped against each edge of the board. The ends of the scrap are set flush with the end of the board. This lets

Always plane in "uphill" direction of grain and planed surface will be smooth.

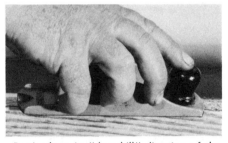

Don't plane in "downhill" direction of the grain. Cutting edge snags grain ends.

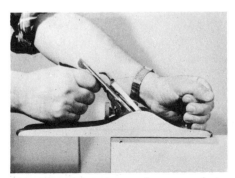

Always keep plane bottom flat on wood at start and finish of the stroke. If plane tilts over end of wood it will round the corners.

To plane end grain without splitting edges, clamp a piece of scrap wood on each side of the work and plane across all three. Any splitting will occur in the scrap, leaving the work smooth and square.

you plane freely all the way across the board end, as any splitting will be in the scrap. The end of the board, itself, will be smooth and square. If you want to plane a bevel or chamfer, just tilt the plane and go to work. A chamfer on the end of a board should be planed with the grain, by angling the plane downward over the corner. The plane cuts more easily in this type of work when it is held at an angle to the direction of travel, so the cutting edge is not straight across the cut.

Plane sizes vary with the job they are designed to do. In general, the longer the plane the greater its edge-straightening effect. If a board edge is bumpy or wavy the long plane rides on the high spots, shaving them down before it cuts the low spots, thus straightening the edge. Some planes were once made 5½′ long for this purpose. Modern lumber processing makes them unnecessary. A short plane rides up and down the waves and bumps, narrowing the board but leaving the wavy edge. On an edge that is purposely curved, the shorter the plane the better.

The Block Plane is the shortest standard form, usually about 6″ in length. Its plane iron is inclined at a shallow angle, usually of about 20 degrees, in some models 12 degrees to ease end grain planing on hardwoods. Because of its shallow angle the plane iron is mounted bevel up, the opposite of other standard planes. It is from this end-grain planing, once commonly termed "blocking in," that the plane gets its name. But it can be used for many small

Block Plane   Jack Plane

Surform tool can be used like a plane on wood, soft metals, and plastics. Blade is simply replaced when dull.

jobs across or with the grain, and is especially handy as it can be operated with one hand while the other hand is free to hold the work.

The Smooth Plane ranges from 7″ to 10″ in length and has its plane iron mounted bevel down. A "plane iron cap" is mounted on top of the plane iron close to the cutting edge to provide a sharper bend and greater breaking effect on the shaving. This minimizes surface roughening when the plane is used to smooth irregular grain areas.

The Jack Plane (once called a jackass plane because of its workhorse use) ranges from around 12″ to 15″ in length, and has the same general features as the smooth plane. Its extra length gives it moderate edge-straightening qualities.

Fore and Jointer Planes range from 18″ to 24″ in length, with features similar to the jack plane. These are the ones to use where edge-straightening is a major aim.

Originally, the jack plane and fore plane had curved cutting edges with a $\frac{1}{16}$″ bulge on the jack plane and $\frac{1}{32}$″ on the fore plane. Today, of course, the cutting edges are straight. The reason: traditional plane features, and those of various other tools, were developed when lumber was commonly sold rough sawed. The curved cutting edge left a wavy surface rather than a sharp outline between plane passes, making final smoothing and finishing easier. Tip: grind an extra plane iron to a curved cutting edge to create a hand hewn appearance on beams.

Electric Planes do much the same type of work as hand planes, usually with a cutter turning at speeds up to more than 20,000 r.p.m. Some are made as attachments for routers. These consist of a plane assembly on which the high r.p.m. router motor can be mounted. This is fitted with a planing blade, often in the form of a rotating spiral cutter.

The Rabbet Plane is used to cut a recessed "step" along the surface of a board at the edge. The cutter extends all the way to the edge of the plane on one side so the plane itself can drop deeper into the wood as the cut progresses. A "fence" or guide attached to the plane rides along the board edge and can be adjusted to hold the rabbet to the width desired.

The Plow Plane, or grooving plane, might be compared to a very narrow plane working in a fixed path along the wood surface. Instead of smoothing the surface it cuts a slot, or groove. A depth gauge and adjustable fence control the depth and path of the cut. The width depends on the width of the cutter used, which usually ranges from $\frac{1}{8}$″ to $\frac{3}{8}$″. Many of these planes are

Rabbet Plane

Imported English Plow Plane

Imported English Circular Plane

Spoke Shave

now imported, like those on the preceding page, from Anglo-American Distribution, Ltd., P.O. Box 24, Somerdale, N. J. 08083.

The Circular Plane has a flexible steel bottom that can be bowed to a wide range of curvatures to fit a concave surface to be planed. An adjusting screw varies the curvature, as required, and holds it as set. Once adjusted to the surface, the plane is used in the normal manner. This is also an import.

The Spokeshave is actually a plane so short it can be used on either concave or convex surfaces. Because it is so short, the handles cannot be placed in the usual position, and are extended from the sides. In use, the spokeshave is usually pushed, rather than pulled, with one hand gripping each handle. In using either the circular plane or the spokeshave, careful attention should be paid to the direction of the wood grain so the cutting stroke can be made in the uphill direction of the grain.

The Modelmaker's Plane is similar to a miniature block plane, typically 3½″ long. It varies in form, but one of the most popular types has a slightly convex bottom, curved both lengthwise and sidewise. The curvature enables

Modelmaker's Plane

Molding planes, now imported, are often made of wood.

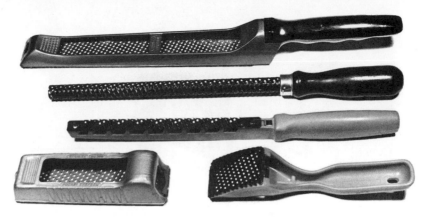

Special-purpose Surform tools, top to bottom: flat and round "files" for enlarging holes; narrow blade for working in slots; pocket plane, left, and shaver for curved surfaces.

the cutting edge to reach into hollows of the work. Widely used by model and violin makers, it is operated like a conventional plane. As its blade is usually more steeply inclined than that of the block plane, it is better to choose a block plane for end-grain work.

The Surform surface-forming tool, though not a true plane in the usual sense of the word, has some unusual advantages. In place of the single cutting edge of the plane iron, this tool has hundreds of tiny individual blades, somewhat like an old-fashioned nutmeg grater. The blades are all level, however, and staggered so that succeeding blades cover the gaps of those ahead of them. The Surform tool is especially well adapted to end-grain work and to rounded forms. For concave surfaces it is made in special curved-blade types. No cutting depth adjustment is required and when the multi-bladed cutting base is dulled it is simply replaced. In use, the Surform tool is handled like a plane. Many forms of the tool are now available.

Molding Planes, the most elaborate of all, now often made of wood, are usually imported. Traditional woodworkers, using as many as 55 different blade forms in these tools, could produce practically every common molding from ordinary rectangular softwood lumber, or duplicate the molding form on the edge of a single panel. It is easy to visualize the principle of the plane's operation if you have ever used an ordinary plane with a nicked cutting edge. A raised ridge appears in the planed surface where the nick passes over it. In similar fashion, the contour of the molding cutter's edge is reproduced in the wood as it moves progressively deeper. Nonstandard molding forms can also be produced by grinding blank cutters to the required edge contour. Adjustable fences are provided on the tool to guide it along the work. Today, the work of the molding plane is often done by the electric router or shaper.

Care of Planes. To protect the cutting edge of the plane iron lay the plane on its side when not in use, or nail a batten along the plane shelf and rest the front of the plane bottom on it to hold the cutting edge above the shelf surface. The latter method conserves storage space. Because of its considerable mass, a large plane is particularly susceptible to rust from condensation in

Plane-iron sharpener clamps plane iron at pre-set angle, holds it there while cutting edge is moved back and forth over whetstone.

Whet plane iron by sliding it back and forth on whetstone while held at whetting angle. Try not to let plane iron rock while whetting.

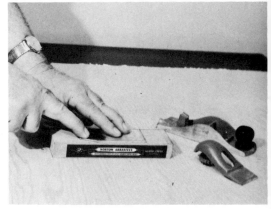

After whetting bevel, slide plane iron back and forth once or twice with flat surface on stone to remove wire edge.

damp, cold weather. Prevent rust by keeping the plane in a heated place or by wiping it with a film of light oil, which can be removed from the bottom before use with a dry cloth.

Sharpening. The same angles and procedures are used in sharpening plane irons as in sharpening chisels. And the same whetting angle guide tool can be used to simplify the work and assure accuracy.

CHAPTER SIX

TOOLS FOR BORING HOLES

AMONG THE HAND TOOLS in the average workshop there are usually at least two capable of drilling holes in both wood and metal. In addition there are likely to be several special-purpose hole-making tools for wood alone. Even though the shop's equipment includes a power drill, the hand-operated types are essential. Some, like the awl, are actually easier and faster than a power tool for certain work. All are handy for jobs where power is unavailable or inconvenient to reach.

The Hand Drill is crank-operated and geared to turn the drill bit three times for each turn of the crank. This provides ample speed of rotation for twist drills in either wood or metal, yet it is slow enough to avoid overheating the bit in metal work. The maximum capacity of the chuck in most hand drills is usually ¼″.

A shallow awl hole makes a good starting point for the bit in wood and assures accurate location of the hole. A center punch indentation does the same in metal. In using the hand drill hold the handle with the left hand, applying moderate pressure *straight* downward. Any tilting of the drill as

Hand Drill

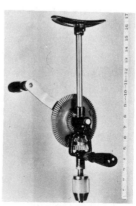

Breast Drill

To drill perpendicular to surface stand a square (or square object) on the work and align tool with it.

Bit brace used with a depth gauge made by boring through piece of scrap wood cut to proper length.

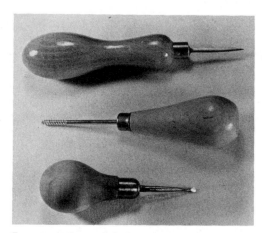

From top: Square shaft awl; threading gimlet; brad awl.

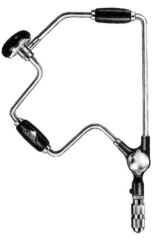

Corner Brace

the bit moves deeper into the work invites bit breakage. To avoid this and the chance of wobbling due to crank action, apply driving force to the crank mainly on the up and down portions of the crank turn. Let your hand "coast" with the crank across the top and bottom of the turn. This is more important with smaller bits than with large ones.

The Breast Drill is a larger form of crank drill with an arched breast plate on top of the handle. This allows the operator to exert greater pressure by resting his chest or shoulder on the plate. Typical breast drills have a twist drill capacity to ½". The Millers Falls 120, shown, has two speeds and can be shifted from 3:1 ratio for small twist drills to 1:1 for large ones in hardwood. A convenient feature on some higher-priced models is an adjustable ratchet on the spindle. This provides either clockwise or counterclockwise motion to the bit when the drill is used in tight quarters where the crank can only be turned back and forth. Even a reversing crank movement as short as 1" is enough to keep the bit turning. The rules for using the breast drill are the same as for the hand drill.

The Bit Brace provides the greatest turning leverage of the hand boring tools. The larger the "sweep diameter" (the circle in which the crank handle turns), the greater the leverage. This averages around 10″ in general-purpose braces, and runs as high as 14″ in heavy-duty models. The maximum diameter of auger bits for the brace is 2″, expansive bits about 2½″. The head, or upper handle, of the brace is centered above the bit chuck in standard types.

The corner brace is a bevel-geared form with the center line of the sweep on about a 45-degree angle to the center line of the chuck. This permits boring close to walls.

The short brace is the smallest of all types, and has no true crank. The cap is mounted directly above the chuck spindle and a short, straight handle extends outward from the ratchet box. The bit is turned by back and forth movement of the handle. This is now usually an imported item.

All through-boring with any bit brace should be done in two steps. Bore from one surface of the wood until the tip of the lead screw emerges from the wood. Then turn the work over and start again with the bit centered in the lead screw hole so the borings meet. This procedure prevents splitting out either surface as the bit comes through.

The Gimlet, in its original form (now imported), resembles a corkscrew, but is straight-shafted and tipped with a small auger bit for boring. Another model resembles an awl, but has a threaded tip like a wood screw. Sometimes called a threading gimlet, it makes a threaded starting hole for small wood screws and is often available in several sizes.

The Push Drill can be operated with one hand while the work is held by the other. A spirally threaded shaft spins the bit several times with a single push stroke. When pressure is released a spring extends the handle again for the next stroke. The maximum diameter of the drill bit is usually around $^{11}/_{64}$″, or a little over ⅛″. This is the tool to use in drilling pilot holes for screws and nails. It uses straight-fluted bits (called drill points) described later.

The Awl is the simplest of hole-making tools and often one of the handiest. The *scratch awl* has a rounded point like an icepick, and is often used as one.

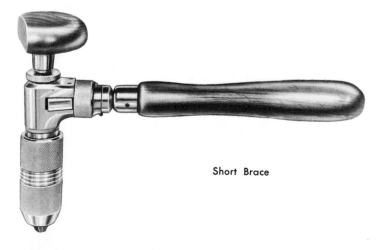

Short Brace

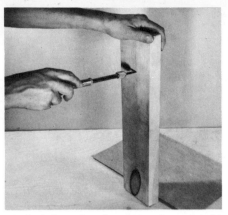

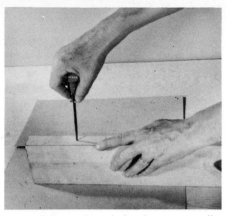

Push drill used with one hand, work held with the other.

Use awl for making holes for very small screws or for starting hole to locate larger bits accurately.

As the name implies, it can be used to scratch a guide line on wood or metal. It is also used to make a center hole for drilling, and a shallow hole for starting small screws. The *brad awl* has a flattened point like a tiny screwdriver, and can be used as one on very small screws like those used in watches and instruments. In woodworking, the sharp, flattened tip is started into the wood with the edge *across* the grain and turned back and forth as the awl is pushed deeper. This severs the wood fibers and permits the brad awl to make deeper holes than the scratch awl (which simply spreads fibers) without splitting.

The Auger Bit for boring wood is available in diameters from $\frac{3}{16}''$ to $2''$ in a variety of types, all suitable to everyday work. The sharp, threaded *feed screw* protruding from the center of the bit is made in *single thread* form (threads farther apart) for fast cutting in green or gummy wood, and double thread form (threads close together) for seasoned wood. The first is best for construction work where wood may be damp or gummy in nature. The second type is preferable for cabinetmaking. Other differences in standard auger bit features are not of critical importance. The size of auger bits is indicated by a single number representing sixteenths of an inch, and stamped on the squared end of the shank. Thus, the number 8 means $\frac{8}{16}''$, or $\frac{1}{2}''$.

Sharpening an auger bit is a simple matter with a small mill file or a bit file made for the purpose. You will notice that the two cutting edges are beveled like chisels on the surface nearest the tang of the bit. File *this surface only* to restore a cutting edge. A few strokes usually do the job. Sharpen the

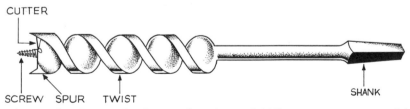

Parts of auger bit: Spurs make downward cut in wood while cutters remove material between screw and spur. The twist carries removed material upward to clear path for cutting.

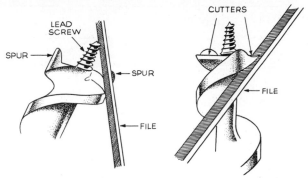

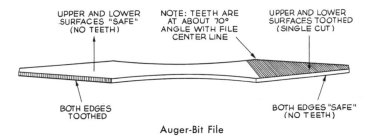

When sharpening an auger bit, sharpen only *inside* of spur edges (left) and never file any part of lead screw. When sharpening cutters (right), file only the surface nearest the shank. Like a chisel, the cutters must have only a single bevel.

Auger-Bit File

spurs by filing on the *inside surface only.* You can give a final keenness to both by whetting with a small slipstone. The job is not critical, but try to keep the edges of spurs and cutting edges even. Don't file heavily on one, lightly on the other.

The Twist Drill is used primarily in drilling metal, but also works in wood. The "lips," or cutting edges, at the entering end are ground to a 59-degree angle on both sides of the center line to form a 118-degree point for average work. A much sharper 82-degree point is used for wood, sometimes a still sharper 60 degrees. Angles for other materials are shown in the chart. The basic grinding idea is that the cutting lips of the drill's entering end be made the "highest" edges. All drill tip surface behind them is ground lower, so only the cutting edge contacts the material being drilled. The trailing edge (behind the cutting lips) is called the heel, and when measured with a drill-point gauge, as in the drawing, is about 12 degrees lower than the lip. The *rake* of the cutting lip is another factor in drill grinding. It is the angle of the undersurface of the lip (resulting from the spiral form of the drill) and can be compared with the angle of a plane iron. For most materials the rake angle is left "as is." But for brass and copper, most plastics and hard steels, the lips are ground to "zero rake." This compares to a plane with its blade set vertically instead of at a cutting angle. It gives a scraping action to the drill rather than a cutting action, and prevents it from "digging in" and breaking, as might otherwise occur in the materials mentioned.

The Expansive Bit has a single-spur cutter that can be extended varying distances from the lead screw to bore holes of different sizes. A typical model like the Russell Jennings expansive bit can take three different cutters. One

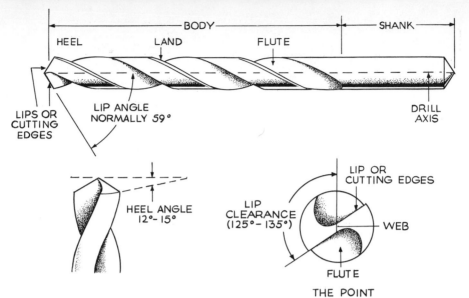

Nomenclature of a twist drill. Lip angle shown is for average work.

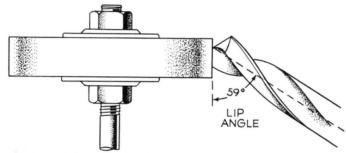

How lip angle of twist drill is ground: Drill is mounted in jig and rotated against perimeter of grinding wheel. Complete sharpening job is easily done with ready-made drill-sharpening attachment which can be set to produce desired angles.

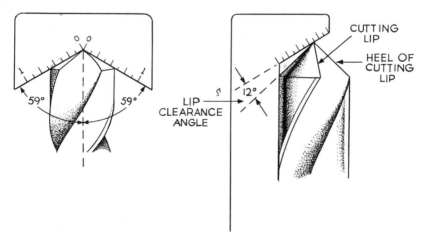

Several types of twist-drill point gauges are available. Type at left fits snugly when applied to cutting lips. Type at right, when applied to the *heel* of the cutting lip, reveals a 12- to 15-degree gap. Either type of gauge may be used to check both edges.

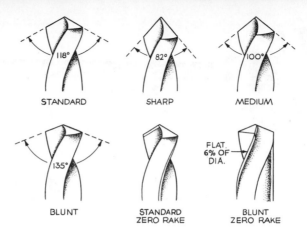

Drill grinding to suit different materials: *Standard grind* suits most materials, especially soft to medium steel. *Sharp grind* is designed for top performance on wood, Hi-silicon aluminum, and thermoplastics. Still sharper 66-degree angle is also used. *Medium grind* works well on Hi-silicon aluminum, is tops on hard copper, cast iron, fiber, and hard rubber. *Blunt grind* is for soft to medium aluminum alloys. Works well in drilling very thin sheets. *Zero rake* is standard and blunt grind is for very hard steels.

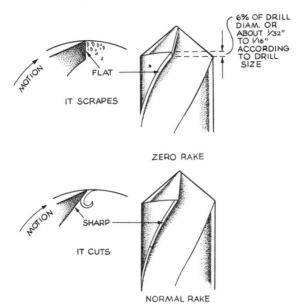

Zero-rake drills are ground with flat edge under cutting lip to produce scraping rather than cutting action, prevent "digging in" on such metals as brass. It also makes a stronger cutting lip for very hard steels.

NUMBER OF SCREW		1	2	3	4	5	6	7	8	9	10	12	14	16	18
BODY DIAMETER OF SCREW		.073	.086	.099	.112	.125	.138	.151	.164	.177	.190	.216	.242	.268	.294
		$\frac{5}{64}$-	$\frac{3}{32}$-	$\frac{3}{32}$+	$\frac{7}{64}$+	$\frac{1}{8}$	$\frac{9}{64}$-	$\frac{5}{32}$-	$\frac{11}{64}$-	$\frac{11}{64}$+	$\frac{3}{16}$+	$\frac{7}{32}$-	$\frac{15}{64}$+	$\frac{17}{64}$+	$\frac{19}{64}$-
FIRST HOLE	TWIST DRILL SIZE	$\frac{5}{64}$	$\frac{3}{32}$	$\frac{7}{64}$	$\frac{7}{64}$	$\frac{1}{8}$	$\frac{9}{64}$	$\frac{5}{32}$	$\frac{11}{64}$	$\frac{3}{16}$	$\frac{3}{16}$	$\frac{7}{32}$	$\frac{1}{4}$	$\frac{17}{64}$	$\frac{19}{64}$
	AUGER BIT NUMBER							3	3	3	3	4	4	5	5
SECOND HOLE	TWIST DRILL SIZE		$\frac{1}{16}$	$\frac{1}{16}$	$\frac{5}{64}$	$\frac{5}{64}$	$\frac{3}{32}$	$\frac{7}{64}$	$\frac{7}{64}$	$\frac{1}{8}$	$\frac{1}{8}$	$\frac{9}{64}$	$\frac{5}{32}$	$\frac{3}{16}$	$\frac{13}{64}$
	AUGER BIT NUMBER												3	3	4

Drill guide for wood screws. *Courtesy Stanley Tool Co.*

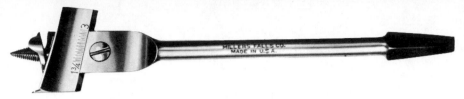

Expansive bit bores holes from 1¾″ to 3″ diameter.

Countersink for bit brace.

Countersink bit for hand or power drill.

bores holes from ⅞″ to 1½″ diameter, another from 1½″ to 2½″, and a third from 2½″ to 3″. A full turn of the adjusting screw enlarges the hole size by ⅛″, half a turn, $\frac{1}{16}$″. In through-boring, a piece of scrap wood should be clamped to the back of the work to prevent splitting when the bit emerges. This bit is a very useful tool that eliminates the need for a large assortment of auger bits.

The Forstner Bit (also called the Foerstner or Fostner bit) has no center point or lead screw. To start the bit you scribe a circle the size of the bit and press the sharp bit rim into it. It is used to drill a hole part way through a board close to the opposite surface where the lead screw of an auger bit would penetrate. The Forstner bit, having no lead screw, leaves the opposite surface unblemished. Like auger bits, Forstner bits are sized by sixteenths of an inch, from No. 4 (¼″) up. These are useful tools in fine cabinetwork.

The Countersink is actually a small conical reamer, matched in form to the angle of flathead screw heads. Turn it a few times in a screw hole, being careful not to go too deep, and it provides a recess so the screw will seat flush with the surface. It is available with shank to fit a bit brace or hand drill.

The Multi-Bore Bit (like the Stanley Screw-Mate) is made with two different diameters along its length, with a conical cutter at the top. The small diameter entering section of the bit drills a hole sized to provide a firm bite for the screw thread. The upper portion drills a larger hole for the smooth screw shank, and the conical cutter at the top countersinks for the screw head, all in a single operation. Another variation of the same bit does all the jobs mentioned and also provides a recess for a wood plug above the countersink. This is the type to use when the screws are to be completely concealed. You can either buy the plugs at a hardware store in wood to match the work, or make your own with a plug cutter bit. These bits are made with a ¼″ shank

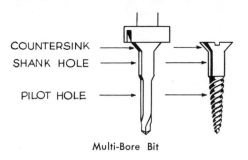

COUNTERSINK

SHANK HOLE

PILOT HOLE

Multi-Bore Bit

to fit a power drill. They are available in sizes to cut ⅜″, ½″, and ⅝″ plugs, the diameters most commonly used.

If you drill holes for screws with standard twist drills, or auger bits for larger screws, select the bit diameters to match the screw size as shown in the chart. A standard countersink bit makes the recess for any size flathead screw.

Drill Points for push drills are long-lasting and inexpensive, so are more often replaced than re-sharpened. If you must re-sharpen one, however, maintain the same point angles. The bits vary somewhat with the manufacturer, but in common form, have a lip angle similar to a twist drill and roughly the same clearance angle. They are straight-fluted, however. Your best guide to re-grinding: examine the largest size drill point and grind any dull ones to match.

Depth Gauges are available to clamp on auger bits and twist drills to serve as a stop against the wood when the bit reaches a pre-set depth. You can make your own by cutting a piece of scrap wood to a length that will reach from the chuck to the desired stop point along the bit. Then drill through the scrap and leave it on the bit, seated against the chuck. When the bit reaches the set depth the end of the wood will act as a stop. Readymade or homemade depth gauges are handy when a number of holes must be bored to the same depth, as in dowel work.

CHAPTER SEVEN

HAMMERS

YOUR CHOICE of a hammer, like any other tool, depends on the type of job at hand. Hammers are specifically designed for various types of nailing, for ripping and prying boards, for driving chisels or pounding joints together, for tacking carpets and upholstery, and for spreading rivets and pounding metal into shape. The right hammer can mean the difference between a bungled and an efficient job. Chóose it carefully.

The Nail Hammer is the best choice for everyday woodwork. It's made in two easy-to-spot types: *curved claw* for general maintenance and cabinet work, and *straight claw* (also called a ripping claw) designed to fit between boards for ripping and prying, as in opening crates or dismantling work. You can drive or pull nails with either one, but the curved claw's "rocker" action offers better wood surface protection in nail pulling because it cuts the chance of denting the work with the other end of the hammer head. Pick a curved claw for your first hammer, a straight claw for a second one if you need it. The second hammer can often be used to "buck" the other side of the work and prevent it from bouncing.

Hickory handles are traditional because they are tough and have shock-

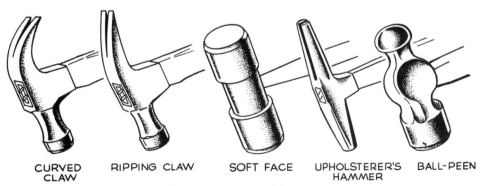

| CURVED CLAW | RIPPING CLAW | SOFT FACE | UPHOLSTERER'S HAMMER | BALL-PEEN |

Five common types of hammers.

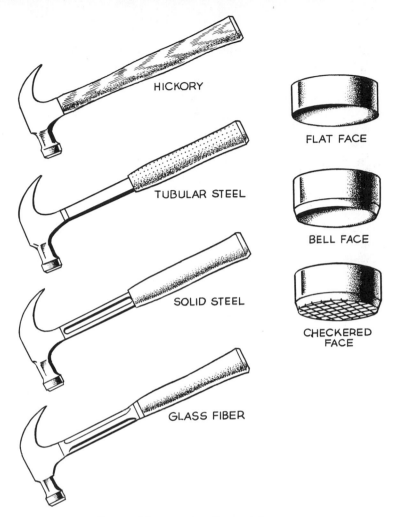

HICKORY

TUBULAR STEEL

SOLID STEEL

GLASS FIBER

FLAT FACE

BELL FACE

CHECKERED FACE

Types of hammer handles and faces.

absorbing resiliency. Wedges driven into the upper end lock the handle so firmly in the hammer's "adze eye" opening that it takes 3 tons to pull the head off a good one. To prevent loosening by dry shrinkage, a hickory-handled hammer shouldn't be stored where it's too hot, as above a workshop radiator. Neither should a good tight-handled hammer be kept where it is wet or overly damp. This swells the already tight handle in the head, crushing the wood fibers against the metal. When it dries it's actually slightly smaller due to the crushed fibers. This can cut "pull-off" resistance from 3 tons to half a ton in twenty-four hours, and sometimes loosen the handle altogether. You can tighten it temporarily by soaking, but it will loosen again when it dries. For protection against this trouble some brands are moisture-sealed. Many are still in use after twenty years without loosening.

Steel handles are made in two types, one tubular and mechanically locked in the head, the other solid and integral with the head in a single forging. Both are free of shrinkage problems and extremely rugged, although you can damage the lighter weight tubular type by a severe blow directly against the handle. It takes close to a 4-ton pull to get the head off a tubular steel handle, 10 tons to break the head from a solid one-piece forged model with an I-section handle. For shock absorption and nonslip hold both types have hand grips of plastic, rubber, or leather. Pick a steel-handled hammer where damp-dry extremes are a problem, and for extra rough use.

Fiberglass handles, the newest type to be introduced, have steel-like strength but look and feel like hickory. The handle is permanently factory-bonded in the head by a pour-in resin that fills the minute space between the handle and the inside of the opening in which it fits, then sets hard. (The same pour-in bonding is also used on some hickory handles, eliminating any strength loss due to wedging.)

Hammer Faces are made with several different types of striking surfaces. Each is designed for a specific task.

The *plain face* is nearly flat and is likely to leave hammer marks if not carefully used, but it's preferred for certain types of work, such as extensive toenailing in house framing. The flat face gives good control in angling the nail at the start, lets you drive it up tight easily where you have to strike the final blows near the rim of the face.

The *bell face* is slightly more convex, can drive a nail flush or even slightly below the surface without leaving a noticeable hammer mark. Properly used it can also do toenailing. Pick a bell-faced hammer for general use.

The *cross-checkered face* has a miniature nonskid tread designed to minimize nail ricochet in fast work like crating and sheathing. It's not suited to general use, leaves a marring imprint, and shouldn't be used on finished wood or cabinetwork.

Hammer Weight, which applies to the head only, is strictly a personal choice. Curved-claw hammers range from 7 to 28 ounces, while ripping hammers usually weigh from 16 to 20 ounces. Handle length, overall, runs from 12″ for a 7-ouncer to 13½″ in the heaviest models.

The best procedure in selecting a hammer is to try several of different weights in your hand, swinging each as you would in actual use. Then pick the one that feels most comfortable and balanced. The generally accepted standard is 16 ounces for everyday woodworking; 10 ounces is a minimum.

Judging Hammer Quality. Some important quality features can be seen, some can't. Look for a *sharp* V-notch between claws for a tight jam-grip on small or headless nails. If you're in doubt, try it. Look carefully for a 2-degree "toe-in" that tilts the striking face of your hammer slightly inward toward you to match the natural arc of your swing and produce squarer hits, fewer bent nails.

Check the end grain of a hickory handle. For peak strength the grain lines of top-quality handles run parallel to the head.

Look also for a smooth finish on all striking surfaces of any hammer, and on the top surfaces of claws, for functional reasons. Extra polished areas add only to appearance. The same applies to an octagonal neck on the business end of the hammer head.

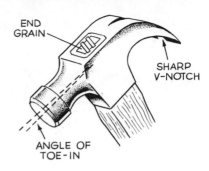

END GRAIN

SHARP V-NOTCH

Features to look for in a claw hammer.

ANGLE OF TOE-IN

Features You Can't See. You can't tell the exact nature of the metal in a hammer head by looking at it, so look for the label, tag, or carton legend that often states the materials used in a top-grade tool.

The head should be drop-forged steel with hardened striking surfaces. It should be softer in the body portion to reduce metal fatigue. Hardness is also purposely lowered to reduce brittleness and to cut the chance of breakage in certain other parts, as in slender claw tips. In some, the rim of the face may not be as hard as the inner area to reduce edge-chipping from misdirected blows.

Your hammer works with greater power than most hand tools. A typical blow delivers a force of 45 foot-pounds, enough to throw a pound weight over a four-story house. Hammer-nail contact pressure may easily top half a ton per square inch, so a hard face is essential, as is a rugged handle. The greatest strain is in pulling nails, not in driving them. If you put a 100-pound load on your hammer handle to draw a nail out of hardwood, leverage boosts that load to around 1,000 pounds near the head.

Soft-Face Hammers are used where finished parts of a project must be driven together, as in assembling a tight joint. They are also handy for driving wood-handled chisels, and for any repair work where a metal hammer might cause damage.

Select a model with screw-on plastic faces that can be replaced when worn badly. Weights range from 1½ ounces to 2 pounds. A 1-pounder is about right for general use.

Magnetic Hammers. Use this type on tacking jobs that call for holding something with one hand, tacking with the other. One end of the head has a narrow slit to form a two-pole magnet that holds the tack point-out on the hammer face. Swing the hammer and you drive the tack. You can pull upholstery taut with one hand, hammer with the other.

With a straight head, tapered at the ends, it's a *magnetic tack hammer* or *bill poster's hammer*. With a longer head, curved downward at both ends, it's an *upholsterer's hammer*. The curve matches the hammer-swing arc, allowing you to drive tacks into a sofa seat close to the back without hitting it and to do other tight-quarters jobs.

Ball Peen Hammers. This is an all-around mechanic's tool, but it is often useful in general shop work. Use the ball end to spread a replacement rivet in cabinet hardware, then "head it over" with either the ball or the face. Weights run from 4 to 40 ounces. Pick a 20-ounce ball peen for average work.

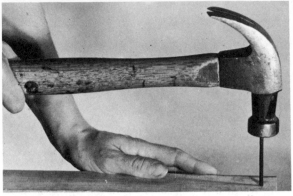 

Hold hammer near end of handle. Keep pivot point of hammer swing at about same level as nail head.

Use nail set to sink finishing-nail heads below wood surface for puttying.

Set block under hammer head for final stage of nail pulling, prevent bending nail and marring wood.

Hold one hammer against nail head while another clinches. This prevents nail head from rising, assures a tight clinch.

Handle length will be around 15 inches. Don't use it as a nail hammer, however, as the face lacks the needed "toe in."

How to Use a Hammer. Hold the hammer handle near the end to provide a full swing arc. Holding it short, nearer the head, results in a smaller arc. This moves the face in a sharper curve and results in glancing blows that bend nails. It also wastes much of the possible force in the swing.

To start a nail into wood hold it with the thumb and index finger of the left hand and give it a light tap or two to stand it up in the wood. Don't slam the nail at this stage; if you miss you'll hit your fingers. Once the nail is started into the wood increase the power of the blows to the full swing, but don't hit so hard you lose directional control. Moderate force drives the average nail

If hammer head is loose, tighten it by tapping base of handle on firm surface.

into most woods with two or three blows. On rough work with common nails finish by driving the nail flush with the wood surface. This sometimes leaves a hammer mark, but it doesn't matter in structural nailing. When using finishing nails, stop when the head of the nail is just above the surface and drive it slightly below the surface with a nail set. This is a tapered tool that seats on the nail head. A tap on the other end of the nail set with the hammer sinks the nail head.

In pulling nails be sure the hammer claws are set snugly against the nail as the pulling begins. The V of the claws can be slid in firmly to grip even headless nails. If the nail is a long one don't try to pull it all the way in a single operation. At the final stage this bends the nail, causing added friction and enlarging the hole left in the wood. It also increases the strain on the hammer handle. Instead, slip a small block of wood under the hammer head for the final stage of the pulling, and the hammer will pull the nail straight up and out.

Care of Hammers. Don't store wood-handled hammers in a hot location, as above a workshop radiator or next to a hot pipe or duct. This can shrink the handle in the head and loosen it. If this does happen, however, soak the hammer, head down, in a bowl of water. Remove it frequently to check on the wood's expansion, and dry it off immediately when the handle is tight. If allowed to remain too long in the water the swelling of the handle will crush the outer wood fibers so the handle will loosen again as soon as the excess water leaves it. In use, strike only with the intended striking surface of the hammer, never with the side, or cheek, the weakest part of the head.

CHAPTER EIGHT

SCREWDRIVERS

FOR MANY A HOME handyman, the screwdriver in the kitchen drawer serves as a kind of do-all tool. He uses it for everything from changing electric plugs to repairing unhinged screen doors. Seldom is he aware that a wide variety of screwdrivers are available, each designed to make a particular chore easier. For occasional fix-it and odd-job work, you can start with two and still cover the range of screw sizes used on most common hardware such as hinges, brackets and latches.

One screwdriver should have a *cabinet blade*—often called an electrician's blade—of ¼" width. The edges of the flat tip of the blade are parallel and the tip width is equal to the diameter of the round section of the shank. It can turn screws in deep holes and recesses. (Deeply recessed screws are most likely to be encountered in this blade width.) For electrical use the round portion of the blade is usually covered with an insulating sheath. To convert an exposed blade for electrical work simply wrap the round portion with vinyl insulating tape.

The second screwdriver should have a standard, or *keystone blade*. The name stems from the shape—wider above the tip, and angular, narrowing back to the round shank diameter. The tip width of this blade should be $\frac{5}{16}$" for general use. The overall length of the cabinet screwdriver should be about 8", the standard one around 10". In use, long screwdrivers are less likely to slip off the screw head than short ones because slight tipping results in less angle variation.

To cover the full range of everyday screw sizes you need five screwdrivers. A given width in these usually means that other dimensions are standardized to match regular screw sizes in that range. But, as some may be found a little off size, a spot check is the best test. The blade tip widths are matched to common screw sizes this way:

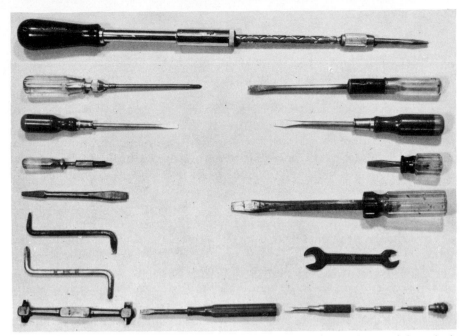

Several popular types of screwdrivers: Top row, spiral ratchet. Top to bottom, left: multiple blade, with chuck to take assorted blades; cabinet; screw-holding; screwdriver bit for bit brace; offset standard; offset Phillips; multi-position offset with four blades at different angles for tight spot work. Top to bottom, right: simple ratchet; standard keystone; stubby; square-shank (to fit wrench below it for high torque); telescoping multiple screwdriver. Successively smaller sizes fit inside larger one.

Blade Tip Width	Screw Size
$\frac{1}{4}''$	6 to 8
$\frac{5}{16}''$	8 to 12
$\frac{3}{8}''$	12 to 16
$\frac{7}{16}''$	16 to 20
$\frac{1}{2}''$	20 to 24

For Phillips head screws you need only four screwdrivers to cover the complete size range, and you'll probably have little use for the smallest size. The screwdrivers and screws match up this way:

Screwdriver Tip Size	Phillips Screw Size
1	0 to 4
2	5 to 9
3	10 to 16
4	18 to 24

The Offset Screwdriver has a lever type of handle which is usually about 4″ to 5″ long. Small as it is, it provides up to ten times the turning power of an ordinary screwdriver. Use it for stubborn screws, such as those locked by corrosion. At one end the blade is parallel to the handle, at the other, at right angles. The two positions permit turning the screw in tight spots where only a quarter turn at a time is possible.

Screw-Holding Screwdrivers grip the screw head with spring steel jaws, holding it on the blade tip. Use this to start a screw in a hole or other location where fingers can't reach. After the screw has been started with a few turns, pull up on the screwdriver and the spring jaws release the screw. The same screwdriver (with jaws retracted) or another can then be used to turn the screw in tight. This type is made in both standard and Phillips form.

The Simple Ratchet Screwdriver provides a continuous turning motion in one direction when the handle is turned back and forth. A slide button adjusts it to turn in either direction or locks it to operate like an ordinary screwdriver. It's easy on the hands as it permits a steady grip on the handle. It's also handy in close quarters where usual hand movement is difficult.

The Spiral Ratchet Screwdriver has all the directional and locking adjustments of the simple ratchet type. But you need only push down on the handle to turn it. The handle itself does not turn, but the spiral ratchet on a typical Yankee model spins the screwdriver bit two and a half times with a single push. A spring then returns the handle for the next push. This is a very handy tool in all screw work, especially where many screws must be driven, as in boatbuilding. Standard bits and Phillips bits in various sizes are available as well as drill bits and countersinks. Socket bits are also made to fit Yankee spiral ratchet screwdrivers to enable them to tighten or remove nuts from bolts.

The Screwdriver Bit for the bit brace is matched to screw sizes and types like ordinary screwdriver blades. It can be used on most work but is best suited to jobs requiring maximum turning force. In the brace, it has the advantage of ratchet operation, if needed, but is slower working than the spiral ratchet screwdriver.

Grinding Screwdriver Blades. Look for a *cross-ground* blade on a standard screwdriver. You can see the grinder marks across the blade in larger sizes, as shown near the tips in the photo. On small blades you can feel it with your fingernail. Tests show that cross-grind serrations bite into the screw slot edges and give 300 percent better holding power than a smooth blade. They actually produce a 20-pound grip on a screw under torque. If you have a smooth blade or if a cross-ground one wears smooth after long use, you can restore the cross-grind serrations with a few strokes across the blade with a bastard file. The file is harder than the screwdriver even if the screwdriver is a hardened one.

Use of Screws. The first step in screwdriving should always be that of drilling a hole to match the screw size. Correctly, the hole should be of two different diameters; the deeper part smaller to give the threads a firm bite, the upper part larger to take the larger screw shank. If a flathead screw is to be used the hole should then be countersunk at the top. Here, avoid the common error of countersinking too deep. Often a turn or two of the countersink is all that is required to allow the screw head to seat flush with the wood surface, as it should. If the screw head is to be concealed by a wood plug the hole for the plug should be the first one bored, equal in diameter to that of the screw head.

CHAPTER NINE

FILES AND RASPS

THE FIRST STEP in filing is file selection. There's a specific file type for each of the common soft metals, for the hard ones, for plastics and for wood. In general, the teeth of files for soft materials are very sharp and widely spaced. Those for hard materials are closer and stockier. The shape of the teeth also differs according to the material to be worked. (In no case are the teeth merely ridges, as they sometimes appear to be. They are actual cutting edges, slanted forward to cut on the push stroke like a saw.) If you use a soft-material file on hard material the teeth quickly chip and dull. If you use a hard-material file on soft material, the teeth clog.

The Cut. File teeth are cut four different ways. A *single cut* file has simple,

Teeth of single cut file showing three degrees of coarseness (from left): bastard, second cut, smooth.

Teeth of double cut file showing three degrees of coarseness (from left): bastard, second cut, smooth.

straight-edged teeth running across it at an angle. This is the type to use where you want a smooth, keen surface, as in sharpening a rotary mower blade. A *double cut* file has a second set of teeth criss-crossing the first ones to form a series of points instead of straight cutting edges. Use this type where you want fast cutting action to remove more material quickly, and where a smooth surface is not important. (If you want the smooth surface too, you can finish with a single cut file.) The *rasp cut* is a series of individual teeth formed separately in manufacture by a sharp, narrow, punch-like cutting chisel. This type cuts the fastest, but it leaves the roughest surface. Use it on wood and other soft materials for fast, rough shaping that will be smooth-surfaced by other means. The *curved tooth cut* is used mainly on metal. (You see files with this cut in auto body shops.) The teeth, though widely spaced, are stocky enough for use on sheet steel as well as on softer metals.

The Coarseness. American Pattern file coarseness is divided into four grades: coarse, bastard, second-cut, and smooth-cut. Swiss Pattern files are used for very precise work and have a different rating system. The coarsest is No. 00, then 0, 1, 2, 3, 4, and 6, the finest. In all files the coarseness is also related to the length of the file. In any grade, tooth size increases with file size, so a 10″ smooth-cut file will actually be much coarser than a 4″ smooth-cut file. The same applies to Swiss Pattern grading.

File Blade Shapes. Files are made with tapered blades and parallel-edged, or "blunt," blades. There are also a dozen cross-sectional forms commonly available, including flat (rectangular), square, round, half-round, triangular, etc. You select the shape according to the job. To enlarge a round hole you use a round tapered file. Use the narrow portion at the start, when the hole is small, the larger portion as hole size increases. (In this type of work keep the file moving around the hole so as not to change its shape.) To file an angular notch, as in sharpening a saw, select a triangular file that fits the notch. For this type of work the file often bears the name of the saw for which it is designed, such as a Cantsaw File. Flat files are for general work, half-round types also handle run-of-the-mill jobs and are more versatile as the curved cutting surface on one side is suited to an additional range of operations.

In a woodworking shop a cabinet file, flat wood file, and half-round wood file should be part of the starting group, all in 10″ length. A half-round rasp, mill bastard, and tapered round file of the same length will also be useful. Another multipurpose form is the shoe rasp, also called a 4-in-hand rasp-file. This has no tang and is not used with a handle. It is half round in cross section with half its length toothed as a rasp on both surfaces, the other half as a double-cut file. As the collection is enlarged, a cabinet rasp is a valuable addition. This is fast cutting but finer toothed than an ordinary rasp, so less smoothing is required after using it. Add others as needed. Your choice is not limited, as there are more than 3,000 types and sizes, among which are the following:

Mill files are used for sharpening mill saws, circular saws, ice saws, machine knives, knives for lawn mowers, axes, and shears. Also made with a single cut

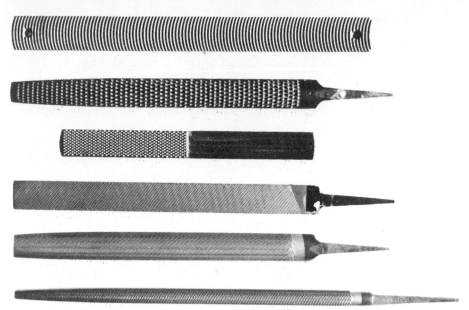

Popular file and rasp forms (top to bottom): curved-tooth file for metal; tapered rasp; shoe rasp; double cut blunt file; half-round file; round file, sometimes called rat-tail file.

for polishing and lathe work where a smooth finish is required.

Special crosscut or mill blunt files are made particularly for filing crosscut and circular saws. Parallel in width and thickness, they are cut like mill files.

Taper files, also called saw files, are used mostly for sharpening saws, also axes, milling cutters, etc. Select one that has a cross section at least twice the depth of the saw tooth. It should be as long as possible to enable you to make steady and effective strokes.

Bandsaw blunt files are used for filing and sharpening bandsaws, and are made so they round gullets between teeth, making the blade less likely to break at the gullet. A sharp angle filed into a gullet becomes a weak point and a likely breaking point.

Crosscut files are used for some types of crosscut saws. The sides are for filing teeth, the rounded back for deepening gullets.

Cantsaw files are used mainly for sharpening circular and crosscut saws with "M" teeth.

Flat files, tapered both in width and thickness, are generally used by machinists. Available in three cuts, bastard, second and smooth, in lengths from 4″ to 18″.

Half-round files are used for fast filing of metal. The half-round back makes it suitable for finishing concave parts as well as flat surfaces. This file may be used on wood as well as metal.

Round files taper to a blunt point and are used for enlarging and smoothing circular openings and curved surfaces.

Three-square files are for general machine shop work, for filing internal angles. Fine for sharp corners.

Square files are generally used for filing keyways, slots and flat surfaces. Also handy for filing flat surfaces of square holes.

Pillar files are for filing narrow slots and keyways.

Warding files are used in making and repairing keys, also for sharpening small twist drills, etc.

Aluminum files are made specially for filing aluminum and its alloys and other soft metals. Tooth construction is such that they will not clog, and will remove material quickly.

Long angle lathe files are used for lathe filing where an extremely smooth finish is desired. Used extensively on soft metals such as aluminum, brass, and bronze.

Flat and half-round foundry files are made with short, stub teeth for general snagging purposes.

Brass files are very sharp with an open cut, are recommended for use on soft metals like copper, brass, and aluminum.

Curved-tooth files are widely used in the automotive industry on aluminum, sheet steel, and babbitt. They easily clear themselves of chips, making for fast work.

Lead float files are available in flat and half-round forms, are used on babbitt, lead, aluminum, brass, and soft metals generally.

Cabinet rasps, as the name implies, are used by woodworkers and cabinetmakers.

Wood rasps, made in flat, half round and round shapes, are used by woodworkers, plumbers, etc. (Slightly coarser.)

Horse rasps are used by horseshoers, have rasp teeth on one side, file teeth on the other. Handy multipurpose shop tool.

Half-round shoe rasps are used in the manufacture and repair of shoes. Half of each surface has file teeth, the other half rasp teeth. Many general shop uses.

Round-handle needle files are used for extremely fine and delicate work, as watchmaking, tool and die making, etc. Made in approximately the same cross-section forms as the larger files, they come to needle points.

How to Use a File. Think of the listed file applications mainly as indications of the kind of work they can do, the work they were designed to do. Then consider the countless applications around the workshop where the same general kind of filing is required. For example, a mill file got its name from its original use in saw-mill work, but it is one of the handiest of workshop files.

The cross-sectional shape of a file is one of the best guides to the jobs it may do. If a round hole must be enlarged a round file does the job, and select one to match the diameter. If you start with a small-diameter file to fit a small hole, you'll have an easier time if you switch to a larger one when the hole is enlarged. This eliminates the scalloped effect of a small file used in different locations around the hole's perimeter. The same applies to flat-surface filing. Use a broad file and keep it moving over the entire surface, not in just one area. This avoids lopsided results. But there are no cut and dried rules except that a file should be used only on the type of material for which it was designed. The rest of the story is common sense and "feel."

Many workers attribute a sort of personality to files. They find that even among identical files, one often cuts faster and more easily in a certain type of material within its range. Minute differences in the files may be a factor, but even a comfortable handle can produce the effect. The trick is in keeping the file cutting, but not forcing it with too much pressure. Either too little or too much tends to dull it, like scraping a knife along a surface instead of letting it cut in, or driving it in with a hammer. If you find a particular file, however, that does a specific job better than similar files in your shop, set it aside for that purpose only. Actually, it's a combination of the file and your individual way of handling it that does the trick. But it pays to maintain a satisfactory match whenever it turns up.

You'll notice, too, that files used on hard materials often work very nicely on soft ones after they have lost some of their original hard-cutting qualities. If a file slows down in its cutting on tough materials try it on something softer —but within its range.

In precision work don't be afraid to use a file with careful, spaced-out strokes. If you want a flat surface keep your file perfectly level as you make the cutting stroke, and don't rush the job. Try the technique on a piece of scrap material and watch the movement of the file and your hands. You may decide to stand in a different position to get the results you need. The idea to overcome (and it's an all too common one) is that the file is basically a "roughing" tool. It isn't. It plays a part in much of the most precise machine and wood work, and it's a very easy tool to control.

To begin a filing job, mount the work to be filed in a vise at about elbow height. (The average workbench vise is about the right height.) If it's a little lower it may make the job easier for heavy filing. Don't hunch directly over the work. Stand back from the vise a little with your feet about 24 inches apart, the right foot ahead of the left. This is a natural stance that allows a comfortable, easy file stroke. Hold the file with the handle in your right hand, the tip of the blade in your left. For average work, the tip is best held with the thumb on top of the blade, the first two fingers under it. For heavy work you'll want to take a full hand grip on the tip.

Apply pressure only on the forward stroke. It's best to lift the file off the work completely on the return stroke, as the teeth will stay sharp much longer. On soft metals, however, the file may be allowed to "drag" lightly on the return stroke, as this helps clear the teeth. (Used properly a quality file remains efficient for hundreds of thousands of strokes, a low-grade one about a tenth as long.) Pay particular attention to keeping the file flat on the work. As your right hand has a leverage advantage at the start of the stroke, and the left hand has at the finish, the file tends toward a rocking motion. Avoid this, as it forms a rounded surface instead of a flat one.

To get the pressure just right, watch the chips. If they are plentiful with each stroke the file is cutting well. You can also "feel" the file bite as you move it forward. With a little experience this becomes the best criterion of the speed of the stroke and the pressure. Both vary with the type of file and the material being worked, but are always moderate. Too little pressure lets

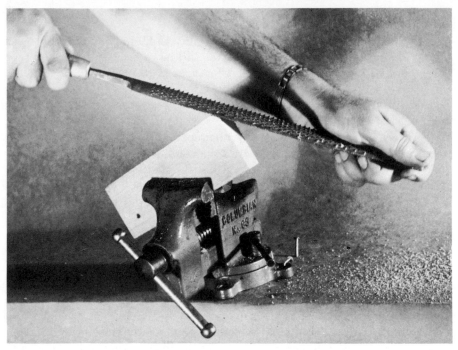

Correct way to hold a file for working wood or metal.

the file skid over the surface without cutting and gradually dulls the teeth. Too much pressure clogs the teeth and results in dulling, sometimes even in tooth breakage.

When a smooth and definitely level surface is required, draw filing is necessary. Instead of pushing the file forward lengthwise to cut, you grip the file at both ends and move it sideways over the work, pulling it toward you then pushing it away with equal pressure in both directions.

Care of Files. Part of the care of files is in their use. Always use the right file for the material being worked. Mount the work firmly in the vise. If it can vibrate it will "chatter" and dull the file teeth. Mount the handle on the file tang by tapping the handle end against the workbench with the file tang in its socket. Never hammer the file to seat the tang. Use the right size handle for the file size. Handles are made in six sizes to fit files from 3″ to 20″ in length, though only the more popular medium sizes are stocked by many hardware dealers. Keep the file clean by brushing out chips, or "pins" as they are often called, with a wire brush called a file "card." A clogged file cannot bite properly and dulls quickly. Store files in a dry place and keep them separated so one will not chip or damage another.

CHAPTER TEN

GLUES AND CLAMPS

THE TECHNIQUE of gluing has changed radically with the introduction of new adhesives. Many of the hard and fast rules of the past no longer apply, and in general the work is easier and the results better. Practically all of the modern wood glues are stronger than the wood itself. Some actually have greater strength when used without the firm clamping that has always been considered essential. Others are so waterproof that boiling or immersing in acid can destroy only the wood, not the glue. And the gap-filling qualities of many of these adhesives assure ample strength in the poorly fitted joints likely in a beginner's work. Because of the problem-eliminating nature of such glues many of the elaborate set-ups are no longer necessary, and simple clamping arrangements can often take the place of costly equipment. So it is wise to familiarize yourself with the glues before selecting your gluing equipment.

Acrylic Resin Glue, such as H. A. Calahan's 3-Ton Adhesive, is packaged in two containers, liquid and powder. Mixing proportions control the setting time. Three parts of powder to one part of liquid give you an average setting time of about five minutes at 70 degrees Fahrenheit. The breaking strength of the bond reaches 3 tons per square inch. This adhesive sticks to almost any material, has been used to splice wooden spars, repair water jackets and crankcases. An excellent gap filler, it is a natural choice where a thick glue line is unavoidable, as it holds better in a thick glue line than in a thin one.

Aliphatic Resin Glue, such as Titebond, a recent development of the Franklin Glue Co., comes ready to use in a squeeze bottle. It looks like heavy cream, but can be pre-colored with water-soluble dyes. Formulated for the furniture industry, it has the characteristic "tack" of the old hot animal glues. A gluing block pressed in place will hold without clamping. On small work, you can hand-hold parts for a minute or two, set the work aside so that the joints stay in line, as the glue stiffens fast. On larger projects, where clamping is a must, clamps can be removed as soon as forty-five minutes after the joint is glued, and re-used on the next joint. Normal room temperature is all that is required. Aliphatic resin glue does not "creep" in joints that take a load.

A gap filler type, it's not waterproof, but water-resistant for indoor use. As it is unaffected by lacquer solvents, fine finishing presents no problem. In the shop, shelf life is a year or more.

Casein Glue, such as Elmer's Casein Glue of the Borden Co., is the old standby in the home shop. A pound can glue just about all the furniture in an average room. It comes in powder form, to be mixed with water. A good gap filler, it can be used at any temperature above freezing. Where maximum structural strength is required for building and construction jobs it is a good choice. Although not waterproof, its moisture resistance is high. Covered bridges built with it in Europe are still in good condition after twenty-five years of use. Shelf life of the unmixed powder is two years or more.

Cellulose Nitrate Cement, familiarly known as household cement can be purchased in tubes and cans. In its clear form it can make repairs that are practically invisible. When amber-dyed, it is easy to see where it has been applied in two-coat work. The solvent is an acetone type, evaporates quickly, brings a joint to 25 percent strength in two hours, full strength (3500 pounds per square inch and over) in twenty-four hours, even in cold weather. Since the solids content is low, evaporation of the solvent causes shrinkage, drawing joints tightly together for a very fine glue line. However this shrinkage can cause distortion on large thin sections.

Hobby shops stock extra-fast-drying types with special solvents. These dry so quickly that you can handle light assemblies a few minutes after gluing, but the fast setting allows less penetration of the wood pores for a firm bond, and thus these cements are not as strong as the regular type. When each surface to be joined is given a second coat of the adhesive over a partially dried first coat, extra holding power results. Although none are water soluble, soaking can weaken the joint.

A good adhesive for repair of porous and semiporous materials, cellulose nitrate cement can also bond nonporous parts provided there is a means for the solvent to escape. Trapped solvent will cause a weak joint, as in large metal-to-metal bonds.

The shelf life of this cement is indefinite.

Contact Cement. As the name implies, this adhesive bonds immediately on contact, and requires no clamps or presses. As formulas vary with different manufacturers, be sure to read the directions on the label before using. Some are flammable, and all fire hazards must be removed—extinguishing pilot lights and following the no smoking rule as when working with lacquer. Some contact cements, such as Weldwood Super Contact Cement, have a water-base and are nonflammable. Both bond instantly with a strength of about 500 pounds per square inch in big areas such as plastic laminate on counter tops. Used to mount room paneling, it eliminates the job of filling nail holes.

Before applying the cement be sure that both surfaces to be joined are clean and dry. On old wood, be sure any paint or previous finish has been removed before coating with cement. Prefit all parts to avoid costly mistakes, as the bond is instant. Both surfaces should have two generous flow-coats, the first coat allowed to dry thoroughly before the second is applied. To test for dryness, press a small bit of heavy wrapping paper to the cemented surface. If no cement adheres to the paper, it is dry. Usually the cement dries in about thirty minutes, longer if necessary, but no more than two hours. Although two coated surfaces will bond instantly, an uncoated surface will not, so use this advantage in aligning your work. Place wrapping paper, as used in the dry-test, between the members until you have a perfect fit, then carefully pull the paper out, and roll the area for a snug bond.

When contact cement is used for applying plastic laminates, large sheets may slip out of line, but this can be rectified. Flush lacquer thinner into the glue line and carefully and slowly peel the laminate free. Continue the flushing process until removal is easy. Clean off any remaining cement with the thinner, recoat the parts, and reassemble.

Brushes and rollers used for coating can be cleaned with lacquer thinner; for the water-base types, soap and water clean-up can be used while the cement is still wet. Shelf life is usually a year at normal room temperature.

Epoxy Glue. Clear or straw colored, this is a two-part resin adhesive. Often labeled "100% solids," epoxy sets entirely by chemical action instead of solvent evaporation, so the whole mixture solidifies. Since there is no problem of solvent evaporation it can be used on large areas for metal-to-metal joints with a grip that can top a ton per square inch. It ranks with the strongest of wood glues, but you would probably be just as well off using one of the less costly glues on wood joints unless there is a definite problem calling for epoxy. China repaired with epoxy glue can be washed in hot soapy water without damage, even be dunked in acid or gasoline. Before it sets it can be easily removed from tools with alcohol or lacquer thinner, even nail-polish remover. It is usable for about two hours after mixing at a temperature of 70 degrees. Tack free in about three hours, it will cure completely in eighteen hours. Quick-setting glues harden in as little as five minutes.

Although epoxy glues are in the top price bracket, they have several distinct advantages. There is no shrinkage because nothing leaves the mixture during setting. It will not soften with heat as it is thermo-setting; it won't "creep" under a steady load; it works almost as well on nonporous materials as on porous ones. For tough jobs like bonding a metal bracket to a slick, polished tile wall, or patching the fiberglass on your boat where the gluing area is too small for other glue, epoxy is the answer. In short, it can be used for repairing almost anything from delicate china to heavy concrete.

Epoxy glues are available in tube size for small jobs. Larger containers for extensive repairs are a good buy as shelf life is usually long at normal room temperature.

Hide Glue. This is the traditional "hot glue" used by old-time cabinetmakers. In flake or strip form you can still buy it at a cabinetmaker's supply house. Its shear strength is rated at a ton per square inch. To use, soak it until it is softened, then heat with just the correct amount of water (check with the manufacturer's instructions as characteristics vary) and use fast so it won't cool and stiffen before the joints are completed.

Liquid hide glue is ready to use, and allows more leeway as it sets overnight. Although not waterproof, hide glue is a strong and time-proven cabinet glue.

Buna-N-Base Adhesive. This type of adhesive, such as Pliobond, is light tan in color and will glue anything to anything, but sets with the flexibility of a kid glove. Made from synthetic rubber, it is available in tubes and bottles. In use on porous materials, the joint can be assembled while still wet. On nonporous materials, you can let it dry, then soften by applying heat just prior to assembling. If you are working on so large an area that the glue dries before you can assemble the parts, reactivate the glue by brushing on the solvent methyl ethyl ketone. Check the manufacturer's instructions for problem applications.

For a strong but completely flexible joint, as between fabric or materials with different expansion rates, Buna-N-Base adhesive is the best choice. One caution—keep newly bonded work off finished furniture as the solvent may cause marring until complete evaporation has taken place.

Polyester Resin Glue. This is another two-part adhesive (liquid resin and liquid catalyst), which must be mixed before use. International Paint Company's Even Flow Resin, made for fiberglass boat work, comes in cans of varying size, and can be pigmented before application. The Vermont Marble Company's Marfix is formulated for repairing marble and stone. Both can be used on wood. Hardening time depends on the amount of catalyst used. During mixing, always be careful to keep the highly flammable peroxide catalyst away from flame (don't smoke), and from contact with your skin. The fire hazard decreases after mixing, and skin contact is so safe that many professional boat workers use their hands rather than brushes to spread the resin. Here, let individual sensitivity guide you, and choose a brush when in doubt. While setting, the resin emits an odor resembling stove gas, but this disappears quickly. Average shelf life is six months.

Polyvinyl Acetate Glue. White when applied, transparent when set, this glue rates high in the furniture industry. It is strong and resistant to impact. In wood joints it becomes hard enough to handle in about half an hour and sets completely in seventy-two hours. Although unaffected by oil, gasoline, and most paints, it is not suitable for use where a lacquer finish is desired, as it is susceptible to lacquer thinner. Essentially an indoor cabinet glue, it is not waterproof or even very water-resistant. However, diluted with water, it makes a durable, protective, clear coating for game boards and maps.

White glue locks conventional wood joints permanently, but should not be used on simple lap joints, as a combination of heat and dampness in the atmosphere can cause it to "creep" under load. It is a fine workshop glue for cabinetwork and porous materials like pottery and leather. Its use on bare metal results in corrosion. Shelf life is indefinite at normal room temperature.

Resorcinol Resin Glue. Another two-part adhesive, this consists of a syrupy wine-colored resin and a catalyst powder. It is completely waterproof and stronger than wood from minus 40 degrees Fahrenheit to temperatures high enough to set the wood on fire. Unaffected by paint, lacquer, gasoline, mild acids or alkalis, even boiling doesn't weaken it. Resorcinol glue sets in eight hours at 70 degrees Fahrenheit, which is the minimum safe working temperature, and in one and a half hours at 100 degrees Fahrenheit. Bond strength continues to increase for almost six weeks. It is a fine choice for boats or outdoor furniture. Shelf life is indefinite.

Rubber-Base Adhesive. Available in tubes for small work, large cans for major jobs, this adhesive sticks to almost anything, and does nonporous bonding as long as there is a way for the solvent to escape. Used with special anchor nails or bolts having large perforated heads, it can secure wall paneling or ceilings to masonry. It is a good caulking material and can be sanded and painted after it is thoroughly dry and hard. It is not flexible like Pliobond.

In boat work, it can actually be applied under water for emergency repairs to leaky seams. It has often been used to seal a cofferdam around a damaged hull section on a large ship, to allow repairs without costly drydocking.

It will stick to anything, but is not recommended for use on wood. On the shelf, it lasts indefinitely.

CLAMPS

Clamps are used to maintain an even and firm contact between surfaces being glued until the glue hardens. The ideal pressure varies with the glue, but can't be measured with ordinary clamping equipment. There is ample leeway, however, so it's a simple matter to judge it from visible evidence. If both surfaces are coated, as they should be, tighten the clamps until an even ridge of glue squeezes out between the surfaces. If excessive glue squeezes out at one portion of the line and runs down the sides of the work, while none squeezes out at another portion, you have uneven clamping pressure or badly matched gluing surfaces. (Uneven clamping pressure is most likely.) Tighten the clamps where there is no squeeze-out, until an even line of glue is showing all along.

To check for excessive clamping pressure apply glue to several scrap surfaces, tighten clamps to bring them together, then open the clamps and examine the surfaces. There should be a glue film over the entire gluing area. If the film is barely visible you have over-tightened your clamps and actually squeezed out so much glue that there may not be enough remaining to make a firm bond. An experiment or two along these lines will give you the "feel" of your clamps. Generally, screw type clamps can apply ample pressure with "finger tightening."

The clamp you'll use most is the C-clamp, but with any metal clamp always use a pad of scrap wood between its pressure surfaces and the wood. The furniture or bar clamp, for wide work, is made in a variety of forms. On some the screw-clamp section is movable, the stationary jaw fixed to the rod or bar. On some, both are movable. In most, the movable jaw locks itself in position automatically as pressure is applied. Simply set the work against the stationary jaw, slide the movable one against the other edge, and tighten.

Adjustable hand screws are sometimes called hand clamps. In their handiest form the screws are threaded into free-turning rods in each of the

C-clamp is most common device for holding glued work under pressure. Use scrap wood under jaws.

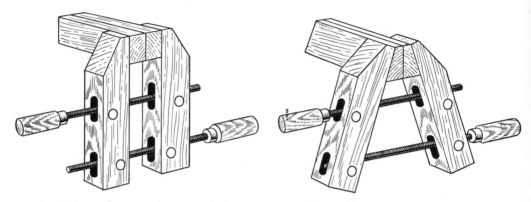

Hand clamps have wooden jaws which may be adjusted to hold angular work. They won't mar surfaces.

Canvas strap on band clamp can be drawn snugly around irregular shapes in unusual gluing jobs.

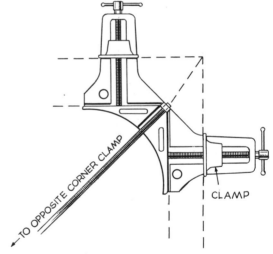

TO OPPOSITE CORNER CLAMP

CLAMP

Corner clamps used in pairs hold opposite sides of miter-jointed picture frame.

Bar clamp has a wide span for gripping glued-up table tops or broad cabinet surfaces.

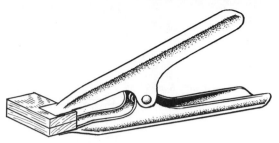

Spring clamp for holding light work under pressure
is handy item in tool kit.

wooden halves so they may be tightened unevenly to clamp angular work. This is a very useful clamp for cabinet work.

The band clamp is similar to the older chain clamp. The band is drawn snugly around irregular shapes to pull all parts together. Then the crank is used to apply final tension. This is the type of clamp to use in gluing hexagonal or octagonal work, for example. It is not likely to be needed for run-of-the-mill jobs.

The corner clamp shown is made by Stanley for miter work. Much simpler to use than older types, it is sold in pairs. In light work like picture framing one pair often does the trick, placed at diagonal corners. For this kind of job the two may be held together by a taut piece of heavy cord. The individual clamps are adjusted to adapt the units to any size rectangle. On heavier jobs two pairs of clamps do the work at all four corners. Small-diameter threaded rods (available at most hardware stores) provide good diagonal tie rods between them when fitted with a nut at each end.

The spring clamp is a quick and effective tool for clamping light work. Simply squeeze the handles to open the jaws, place the work between them, and allow the jaws to close on it. The spring that closes the clamp provides ample pressure for light work.

For occasional wide work you can make your own clamping arrangement. Simply place a 2-by-3 under the work to be clamped with several layers of tissue paper between it and the work. (The paper prevents the glue from

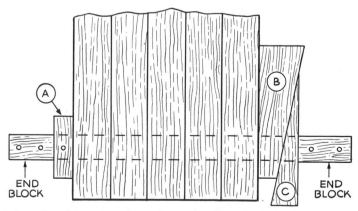

Improvised clamp for gluing up stock can be made of length of 2-by-3 and wooden wedges.

Loop of rope twisted with a stick is a good makeshift clamp for repairing a chair rung.

bonding the 2-by-3 to the work. Nail a short block of 2-by-3 atop the main piece at each end, parallel to it. At one end nail an additional piece crosswise, as at *A*, to act as a pad against the work. At the other end use an inner wedge *B* against the work, and drive an outer wedge *C* between it and the end block to apply pressure. The two wedges, cut at matching angles, provide a firm lateral pressure. This is a handy setup for edge-gluing when you don't happen to own a readymade furniture or bar clamp suitable for the job.

Another useful gluing makeshift is a loop of cord or rope twisted with a stick. This is particularly suited to furniture repairs in which rungs must be held in position until glue sets. Watch the joints as you twist the cord. When they are snug, slip the stick over a rung or use another stick to lock it. Don't apply more pressure than necessary, as you may break the cord.

CHAPTER ELEVEN

COATED ABRASIVES

FOR FINAL FINISHING, use of the proper abrasive gives the home shop project the professional touch. The different types are suited to different materials and kinds of work. Grit sizes and types apply generally in hand or power sanding, although the backing may be paper for hand work, and cloth for a power job.

Flint Paper. This is what most people think of as "sandpaper" although the abrasive is actually white quartz. This has a short working life, so use it when the work will clog the paper quickly, as in hand sanding off old paint, or working on gummy woods.

Garnet Paper. Harder and sharper than flint, garnet is a natural choice for woodworking. Available in a wide range of grits, and with extremely flexible backing, it is suited to fine wood finishing in the shop.

Aluminum Oxide Paper. When there is a lot of stock to be removed from hardwood, aluminum oxide paper fills the bill. Tough and long wearing, it is also used for cutting into hard metals such as steel or iron.

Emery Paper. This is an old stand-by used more for polishing than cutting or grinding, as it is not as sharp as aluminum oxide or silicon carbide. Use it to keep tools gleaming and rust-free.

Silicon Carbide Paper. This is the material to use on soft materials like aluminum and bronze, as its long cutting edges are too brittle for use on hard stock like iron or steel. This is also the abrasive to use on glass, stone, leather and plastics.

GRADING CHART FOR COATED ABRASIVES

	Silicon Carbide	Aluminum Oxide	Garnet	Flint	Emery
Very Fine	600				
	500	500			
	400	400–10/0			
	360				
	320	320–9/0		7/0	
	280–8/0	280–8/0	8/0–280	6/0	
	240–7/0	240–7/0	7/0–240	5/0	
	220–6/0	220–6/0	6/0–220	4/0	
Fine				3/0	
	180–5/0	180–5/0	5/0–180		3/0
	150–4/0	150–4/0			2/0
				2/0	
	120–3/0	120–3/0	3/0–120		
				0	0
	100–2/0	100–2/0			
Medium				½	½
	80–0	80–0	0–80		1
				1	1½
	60–½	60–½	½–60		
					2
	50–1	50–1	1–50	1½	
Coarse				2	2½
	40–1½	40–1½	1½–40		
				2½	
	36–2	36–2	2–36		
					3
	30–2½	30–2½	2½–30	3	
Very Coarse	24–3	24–3	3–24	3½	
	22–3¼				
	20–3½	20–3½	3½–20		
	18–3¾				
	16–4	16–4			
	14–4¼				
	12–4½	12–4½			

Sanding Technique. Whenever possible sanding motion (hand or power) should be parallel to the wood grain. This assures that any marks left by the abrasive will line up with the grain and be less detectable. It also minimizes the tendency of coarser abrasives to tear surface fibers and roughen the work.

There are numerous instances, however, where sanding parallel to the grain is impractical or impossible. When sanding must be done across a mitered joint, for example, the abrasive must move at an angle across the grain of one or both sections. Here, it is very important to progress from one degree of coarseness to the next without skipping, and to "blend out" the sanding as you work away from the miter area. When the work reaches the final stages the very fine grits eliminate the effects of cross sanding for all practical purposes. The same effect is apparent both in hand sanding and in the use of rigid disk rotary sanders and orbital sanders. If the work is to be stained take plenty of time with the final fine-grit stage. The problem to avoid is uneven stain absorption. Cross-sanded areas tend to soak up more stain, take a darker tone. (In orbital and rotary sanding the tone is even over the entire sanded area, as the motion is the same on all parts.)

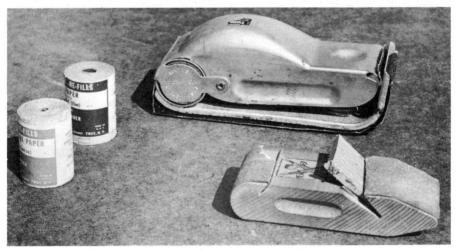

Hand sanders using rolls of coated abrasive help speed work. Metal-bodied sander at top houses abrasive roll in end receptacle. Lower sander, of wood, holds ends of abrasive strip in slots with aid of wooden wedge.

Plain sanding of flat surfaces should be done with the abrasive wrapped around a wood block when you want to even off minor surface irregularities. If you are not aiming to produce a truly flat surface, as in refinishing certain types of Early American furniture with a characteristic waviness of surface, place a felt or thin cellulose sponge pad between the abrasive paper and the block. This provides enough "give" to follow the mild surface contours without sanding entirely through high spots.

Rounding corners is best accomplished with a similar pad between paper and block. Tilt the block to about 45 degrees over the corner and sand with the grain. The give of the felt or sponge produces a truly rounded corner, not a beveled one. If a corner is to be rounded from edge grain to end grain allow the abrasive to move only from edge grain toward end grain, when sanding by hand. Motion in the opposite direction tends to fray out surface fibers. When doing any type of corner-rounding with an orbital or rotary sander use only medium fine and fine paper.

Squaring corners. If you want to retain sharp corners when sanding edge or end grain clamp thin pieces of scrap wood flush with the corners over which the abrasive will pass. This prevents "rocking" of the sanding block or power sander, leaving the corners clean and sharp.

Sanding carved work calls for some ingenuity in adapting the method to the job. In general, sanding cloth is preferable to paper-backed abrasive in this type of work. When it is necessary to reach into crevices of the carving, crease the cloth, abrasive side out, over a dull table knife and work it like a thin file. On "corkscrew" lathe-turned table legs use strips of the abrasive cloth and work in "shoe-shine" fashion. Although this amounts to cross-grain sanding, the original sanding on this type of work was also done that way in the lathe.

Abrasive-fitting, as in giving the final touch to boards that will be edge-glued, is a simple process. Fold a sheet of medium-grit aluminum-oxide paper, abrasive side out, and slide it back and forth between the boards at the location of any high spots. The boards should be held together lightly by a helper during the job. A few strips of scrap wood under the boards will hold them high enough from the floor. Even if the abrasive paper travels considerably beyond the high spot it will do little cutting in the wrong area as pressure is greatest at the high spots. A few strokes are often all that is required to produce a near-perfect fit.

Final surface sanding. For the smoothest possible result in finish sanding, give the surface a single coat of well-thinned shellac after preliminary fine sanding. The shellac stiffens tiny surface fibers making it easy for the next fine sanding to remove them, producing a super-smooth surface. But be sure the shellac has dried thoroughly before the re-sanding.

Making glass edges safe. If you have a large amount of newly cut glass to handle, as in replacing a number of cracked window panes, use waterproof aluminum-oxide or silicon-carbide cloth. Wet the abrasive thoroughly and slide it along the glass edge with the cloth held rounded so as to contact the corners of the edge. Three or four strokes are usually enough to safely dull the sharp corners. If the glass is to be used for a table top or for any purpose where the edge will be permanently exposed, continue the process to remove irregularities and produce a frosted effect. The water lays the dust and helps the cutting action of the abrasive by preventing clogging. A medium grit does the trick. If waterproof abrasive cloth is not available, various types of abrasive paper, including garnet, may be used dry. Use a cloth pad behind the paper, however, just in case the glass cuts through before the abrasive dulls the edges.

Producing a soft luster on a furniture finish is a job for powdered abrasive such as powdered pumice or rottenstone. There are several methods of using these materials, all easy. For one, you may mix them with water to form a thin paste, then rub the paste over the surface with a soft cloth pad. On non-waterproof finishes like shellac, however, No. 10 engine oil is preferable to water for making the paste. The pumice cuts faster than the rottenstone but increases the risk of "rubbing through" the finish. To avoid the chance of a rub-through wipe the surface clean after a very brief period of rubbing. Most first-timers are surprised to find how fast the process works.

Another method consists of placing the powder dry in a shallow pan, and patting a damp cloth pad in it to pick up enough powder to treat an area at a time. This gives you a good view of the results as the work progresses but calls for care to avoid unevenness in luster.

Choosing the Right Grade. If you start with rough wood you'll need grit size No. 1 or ½ for the first stage. If the starting surface is fairly smooth like most dressed lumber you can begin with 2/0 paper. The second stage then calls for 3/0 paper, and the final stage, 5/0. It's usually safe to skip from 3/0 to 5/0, but never skip more than one grade, as from 2/0 to 5/0. If you do you'll find it close to impossible to remove the coarse grade's scratches with the fine grade.

For sanding between finish coats, use 9/0 waterproof garnet or silicon-carbide paper. Use mild soapy water and dip the paper often. Wipe the work dry frequently to prevent water stains. And never tackle between-coat sanding until you are certain the finish has dried thoroughly.

To get the most out of abrasive paper use a type that suits the job. On gummy wood or heavy paint use open-coat paper to minimize clogging, and begin with a coarse grade if much material must be removed. When the paper clogs with dry material in ordinary work, slap it against a hard surface like the workbench top, abrasive side down. This usually clears most of the clogging material from it and gives it a new lease on cutting life.

Part II

CHAPTER TWELVE

PLANNING THE POWER TOOL SHOP

POWER TOOLS literally transform the odd-job home workshop to a little private factory. And it will function more smoothly if you plan it like one: Equip it with tools to suit the type of work to be done. Don't clutter limited space with equipment that won't be used.

Layout. One of the primary factors in shop layout is an easy path for materials coming in and finished projects going out. In the typical basement shop the stairs leading to the outside are often the most convenient route in both cases, as inside basement stairs are often narrow, frequently with a right-angle turn. You may find it difficult or impossible to take a 4-by-8 panel down them, or a completed hi-fi cabinet up. But the panel passes easily down the outside steps and the cabinet can go out that way, then come in the front or back door of the house. Also to be considered in basement workshop planning are the lally columns (round metal supports) spaced out under the girder that runs along the center line of most basement ceilings. If your shop will be partitioned off from the rest of the basement, and if you plan night work, do not attach a partition wall and definitely not a workbench to one of these columns as they will transmit vibration through the house structure. More about noise-stopping later.

Do not confine yourself to ready-made door sizes in planning a partitioned shop. A 4' wide door of ¾'' plywood will give you ample clearance for most materials and projects. If there isn't room to swing such a door make it a sliding door with tracks and rollers made for the purpose, and widely used on large closet doors.

Stationary power tools. Most of the so-called stationary power tools should actually be mounted on braked casters, preferably with rubber-tired wheels. These are a standard item at large hardware stores. In typical form they look like ordinary casters except for a lever running fore and aft across each hub. Push one end of the lever down with your toe and the wheel is locked. Push the other end down and you release it. This allows you to move the power tool to the best location for the work at hand, and lock it there. To handle long work on the table saw, for example, you might want to move it in line with the shop doorway so the work could be led in through the door, allowing maximum shop width for it to pass over the saw. The rubber-tired wheels do two important things. They make a nonskid floor contact and they absorb much of the vibration that might otherwise be transmitted to the floor. The less vibration transmitted from the tool the less is likely to reach the house structure.

The drill press, radial-arm saw, jig saw, bandsaw, and lathe are usually placed along the walls. For most work they can be used without moving them. The reason for making them movable is that there are likely to be many times when part of a partially completed project is so shaped as to jut out behind the tool. To provide needed clearance the tool must be moved out from the wall.

The table saw is often left near the center of the shop and moved elsewhere only when necessary. Placing it in the shop center allows clearance for most ripping and crosscutting as well as the more complex operations likely to be done on the tool.

Walls and Ceiling. If budget permits it is wise to panel the shop walls with inexpensive plywood. This can be nailed to 1-by-4 or 2-by-4 vertical furring strips which can be fastened to the wall with suitable masonry fasteners. The plywood walls should stop short of the wooden ceiling framework if noise control is important. The reason: plywood walls make it easy to mount shelves and tool racks on the wall, but the noise of tools being removed and replaced would be transmitted through the house structure if the wall panels joined the ceiling framework. The same applies to a partition wall. The gap between the top of such a wall and the ceiling can be small and should be filled in with soft fiberglass or felt to stop sound transmission through either air or structure.

For maximum sound insulation the shop can have its own ceiling across the top of wall paneling, completely independent of the existing ceiling. This forms what is literally a room within a room, the type of structure used in laboratories where sound control is essential. An inner surface of acoustic tile and an overlay of fiberglass blanket on top does the rest. Partition walls in this type of structure are made with staggered studs (posts) so that the outer wallboard is mounted on one set of alternate studs, the inner wallboard on another. Vibration from one surface is then not transmitted directly through to the other. There are still more elaborate methods of blocking noise, but these measures are enough for most nighttime workshops, and much more than usually used. The principles involved, however, are worth knowing, as all contribute to confining workshop noise.

Simple Noise-Cutting Tips. Keep the workbench, wall paneling, and all power tools well clear of all pipes. Even a slight tap or vibration against a pipe is carried almost instantly throughout the house. If you have an old carpet use it on the workshop floor. Power-tool casters will roll over it. The carpet reduces reverberation within the shop, thus cutting noise at the source, and also muffles the sound of tools or materials accidentally dropped.

Tools that are bench mounted (like a bench grinder) and bench-mounted motors can be quieted with rubber mountings. Some motors have them built in, but you can always use rubber auto-engine mountings for the purpose. These are made in a wide variety of forms but the general construction is the same. A metal plate threaded to take a bolt (or made with a bolt welded into it) is bonded to a synthetic rubber block, and a similar metal plate is bonded to the other side of the block. The rubber isn't soft enough to allow bounce or wobble, but it's soft enough to absorb vibration. Use the blocks with one side bolted to the bench, the other to the motor or bench tool. Examine a few mounting types at an auto-parts dealer and select the type that suits your needs best.

To give yourself a demonstration of the effectiveness of the principle of cushion-mounting turn on your power drill and lay it on a table or workbench. A sound-level meter will show it to be turning out about ninety-nine decibels—enough to rate it as a noisy tool. Slip a sponge-rubber kneeling pad under it and the level drops to eighty-six, a very great drop in terms of decibels. (They're logarithmic sound-level units). Lay a folded blanket or pillow over the drill and you cut the sound to around seventy-seven decibels. Now you can just about hear it across the room. With the kneeling pad you stopped the drill from transmitting vibration structurally, from using the table or workbench as a sounding board. With the blanket or cushion you muffled the vibrations from its own shell. Your car uses the same basic methods to produce the quiet ride you are accustomed to. And they can be applied to many workshop tools and operations.

If you are sawing a large panel, for example, cover as much area of it as possible with old blanket or quilting. This will stop it from acting as a sounding board. (Musicians sometimes muffle their drums in similar fashion.) If you are sawing by hand hold the saw at a flatter angle to the surface of the wood to reduce noise. And favor a fine-toothed saw over a coarse-toothed one.

Plan your work so noisy operations are done early when the background noise level is high. The normal background noise of a city is around seventy decibels, an average conversation rates around fifty. So a little workshop noise won't be noticed. But at night when you can hear a cat purring at twenty-five decibels, it's too quiet for nailing, so switch to the screwdriver. Or use a familiar sound like radio or hi-fi music playing medium soft as a camouflage. The human ear is less sensitive to sleep-breaking sounds when a familiar sound maintains a background level. But don't key the household to listen for workshop noises by suggesting that they may occur. Thus alerted, the ear picks up noises that would otherwise be ignored.

Different Shop Locations. In the house without a basement the shop is likely to be either in a part of the garage or in a first-floor room, such as a den. The concrete floor of the garage is less likely to send shop noises through the house structure than the wood floor of a den. If the entire house is built on a slab, however, and if the slab is tiled to serve as the ground floor, one is as good as the other. In the garage, be sure that sufficient heat is provided to prevent condensation on tools in damp winter weather. This is most likely to occur with sharp temperature changes, as from a sunny day to a cold night.

If the shop is in an outbuilding like a shed or separated garage, tool noise becomes a minor, if not negligible, problem. Heat, however, may present some difficulties to the uninitiated. As it is seldom feasible to run ducts or piping to the outside garage, a space heater is the best answer. Vented gas heaters that completely seal off all flame from the interior are available, but may not be economical in cold areas not served by gas mains. Here, electric heating is often the simplest answer if the shop is well insulated and has adequate wiring. A small thermostatically controlled electric heater might be used to keep the chill off the shop, plus a wood stove for full heating during periods when the shop is in use. To cut costs, scrap wood from woodworking projects can supplement purchased fuel.

The Apartment Shop is the problem shop both from the standpoint of noise and of space. The portable power drill and its accessories usually provide the best solution to the space problem and go a long way toward solving the noise problem as well. (See Portable Power Drills.) Because the kitchen counter is roughly at workbench height the kitchen or kitchenette frequently becomes an off-hours workshop, but has the disadvantage of transmitting sounds through the plumbing, unless a counter section is separated from that containing the sink. The best bet for the average apartment shop in limited space is a sturdy table to serve as a workbench. Several simple measures may be employed to protect the table and minimize noise. Set the table legs in rubber furniture cups. Cover the tabletop with ½″ foam rubber of the type used as a subsurface layer in upholstering, and lay a table-sized piece of ½″ or ¾″ plywood on top of it. Both rubber and plywood may be stored in the back of a closet when when not in use. If a vise is used the plywood should overhang the table edge far enough to admit the vise clamp. To prevent the plywood from slipping during such operations as planing (the rubber friction will hold it for most other jobs) it can be cinched down with a canvas luggage strap and buckle. Methods for diminishing noise level outlined previously should be applied, with special attention to background noise level. Time the work to take advantage of it.

CHAPTER THIRTEEN

THE PORTABLE POWER DRILL

A ¼″ PORTABLE POWER DRILL lets you bore holes more than twice as fast as you can by hand. It takes the average worker about a quarter of a minute to bore a ¾″ hole through a fir 2-by-4 with a bit and brace. With a power drill he can do it in a little over six seconds.

In the popular sizes, modern power drills can do much more than bore holes. With a typical kit of accessories the basic power unit can be adapted in a minute or two to operate as a sabre saw, circular saw, electric plane, disk or orbital sander, buffer-polisher, and power grinder. The compactness of the accessory group makes it an ideal power tool set-up for the shop that must function in very limited space. As a single power unit is used for all the types of work, however, caution is required to protect it from overheating, especially on long-run operations like sanding. In most cases this can be done by placing a hand on the motor housing. On the average model this is warm to

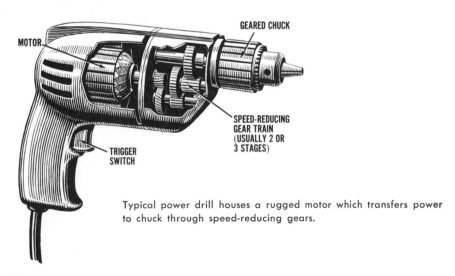

GEARED CHUCK

MOTOR

SPEED-REDUCING GEAR TRAIN (USUALLY 2 OR 3 STAGES)

TRIGGER SWITCH

Typical power drill houses a rugged motor which transfers power to chuck through speed-reducing gears.

the touch in normal operation. But when the temperature begins to rise from warm to hot the drill should be shut off immediately and allowed to cool. Cooling can be hastened greatly by placing the tool in the refrigerator. But don't place it in the freezer, as the extreme temperature differential can cause damage to some units, particularly to certain types of plastic parts. If the multipurpose kit is to be used in extensive work its useful life can be very greatly lengthened by adding an extra power unit. Thus, one can be shut off for cooling while the other goes into action running the same accessory. In many cases, one unit may be left attached to a frequently used accessory while the other is used for varied jobs.

Drill designs have a lot in common regardless of size and make. All are geared down so the chuck runs at efficient drilling speed while the motor turns much faster for peak efficiency. Some, more expensive drills are built with a speed control to match r.p.m. to job requirements. This is more important in extensive metal drilling than in woodwork, as the fixed-speed drills that make up the majority operate at a speed well suited to woodwork and related light metal drilling.

Drill size is commonly rated on the basis of the maximum-diameter bit the chuck will accommodate. The ¼" drill is still the most widely used, and is adequate for most workshop jobs, but the ⅜" size is gaining because its greater capacity and power widen the range of accessories that can be used with it.

The operating r.p.m. of power drills varies with make, model, and size. In ¼" size, typical "no load" r.p.m. is commonly in the 1700 to 2250 range. Full load r.p.m. would then be around 1100 and 1500 respectively. The higher-speed range is good for operations like sanding. The lower range is better for drilling metals like iron and steel. In ⅜" size, the operating r.p.m. is usually lower, typically around 1000 with no load, 650 to 700 with full load. Variable-speed drills in both sizes usually operate at any r.p.m. from 0 to the maximum

Chart plate on housing of ⅜" portable drill lists drilling speeds for different materials according to drill diameter. Dial adjusts drill to desired speed.

Used in drill-press attachment, tool can drill perpendicular to work surface or at pre-set angle when work is held by vise.

listed on the specification plate, but check when you buy, as some have several fixed speeds. The specification plate on many drills, however, lists only the no-load speed. Typically, you can estimate the full-load speed roughly at about a third less. But for average workshop jobs, especially in woodworking, a specific r.p.m. is seldom required. If the drill has variable speed, the chart on page 142 can serve as a guide. A reversible drill is useful in "backing out" twist bits from heavy timber.

The Drill Press Attachment for the portable power drill is a very useful accessory as it makes precise perpendicular drilling easy, and allows wobble-free application of drilling pressure. With the aid of a drill press vise or jigs it also permits drilling at pre-set angles. Because of its light weight, it can also be used in ways an ordinary drill press cannot. For example, if a perpendicular hole must be drilled through the mid-area of a large panel, the drill press attachment can be set in place on the panel with the drill press "head" containing the power drill swung out behind the base. This way, the drill can be brought down to the panel surface to drill through it. The base, on which the work is usually placed, serves simply to hold the drill perpendicular to the surface being drilled. (Unlike the large conventional drill presses, the base and table are one and the same in this type.)

The Sabre Saw Attachment is another handy workshop tool, capable of all the usual sabre saw cuts, though it may be slower in ¼″ drill size. Most present models are locked rigidly to the drill body when in use, so the entire unit can be operated with one hand. This leaves the other hand free to steady the work, a convenience not possible with some of the loosely linked earlier models.

The Circular Saw Attachment is generally limited to a 6″ diameter blade or less. This is adequate for easy through-cutting of nominal 1″ stock, and in

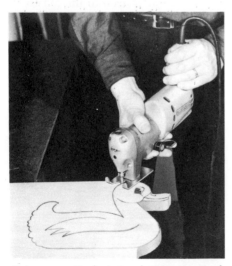

Sabre-saw attachment enlarges range of power drill. It is guided by right hand, left hand remaining on drill handle to operate trigger switch.

Circular-saw unit with 5½″ blade can be set for angles from 90 to 45 degrees. Combination blade is used here in making a beveled rip cut on a pine board.

On extensive sanding jobs, abrasive disc is used with drill trigger button-locked to keep motor running without finger pressure. Check temperature of drill body with hand at frequent intervals.

Bench-sander attachment with tilting table and miter gauge does regular sanding, also precision trimming and fitting. Sanding plate is driven directly off drill spindle.

the larger (6″) size, 2″ stock, such as 2-by-4s. Most models, however, are not designed to make the 45-degree angle cuts through 2-by-4s possible with conventional portable circular saws. This is a relatively minor limitation in general shop work, particularly if cabinetmaking projects are a major aspect of it. But don't force the circular saw attachment in cutting. Remember that even larger models seldom exceed one-third horsepower compared to one or more in the conventional units.

The Plane Attachment, one of the more recent power drill accessories, uses a spiral tool-steel cutter turned by the power unit. In its usual form it can plane an edge as wide as 2″. Depth of cut may be set from 0 to ⅛″ in typical models. While this tool can be used for a wide range of planing operations, it is particularly handy for trimming relatively light structures like screens that might be distorted by the pressure required for hand planing. Simply hold the power plane snugly against the work and move it forward. The cutting action is provided by the rapidly rotating spiral cutter, not by the forward motion, so no heavy loads are imposed upon the work. The tool can be used to plane edges square or bevel. In some models, like the Millers Falls Quik-Change, the bevel range is 130 degrees. Yet the plane unit costs only about a fourth as much as a complete electric plane.

Sanding Attachments. One of the power drill's earliest attachments, the *disk sander,* is fast-cutting and flexible, suited to rapid rough-cutting and rough-shaping of wood. It is difficult to use for finish sanding, however, except in the hands of an experienced worker. (For details see Chapter 16, Power Sanders.)

The rigid disk or sanding plate attachment is usually built into a small sanding table to form a bench sander when coupled to the power unit. This type of sander can do many of the jobs handled by a jointer-planer, but at a slower speed. It can do precision trimming, for example, on either squared or beveled work by taking fine sanding cuts in series. And, in quality models it can even handle compound angles with its graduated angle gauge, similar to the miter gauge of a circular table saw.

The orbital sander attachment, like the conventional orbital sander, is a finishing tool to be used where grain directions change in a joint like a miter. The orbital motion blends the sanding action over the juncture.

The buffer-polisher, another early attachment, is most commonly in the

Orbital sanding attachment permits finish sanding close to corners. This one takes standard abrasive sheets cut in thirds.

form of a lamb's wool bonnet drawn over the same rubber disk as used for the flexible disk sander. (For special work, as in jeweller's rouge polishing, a rag wheel is sometimes used.) The bonnet provides a fast and easy way to bring wax to peak luster on furniture and on small floor areas.

Special-purpose Attachments for the power drill range from paint mixers to hedge trimmers, but are not available for all makes. To be sure of the accessories required for the type of work planned, it is necessary to check the various kits.

If you already have a drill for which certain desired accessories are not specifically made, check over those made for other drills. Many are made to fit practically any model. If accessories are a major factor in your choice of a drill, these all-model attachments may also solve the problem when a particular unit is not available for an otherwies suitable drill.

How to Use a Power Drill. Although a lightweight power drill can easily be operated with one hand, it is better to grip it with both when it is not necessary to have one hand free to grip the work. Use the right hand to apply moderate pressure to the drill in boring and drilling, the pressure being applied through the drill handle. Use the left hand to grip the drill body and act as a brake to check the drill if it penetrates the work suddenly. The two-hand grip also steadies the drill to prevent wobbling, one of the common causes of bit breakage.

In general, it is wise to use high-speed drill bits in preference to carbon bits in metal drilling as they can be run longer and at higher speeds without fear of burn-out. In all metal work except on cast iron (which has a built-in lubricating effect) it is a good idea to apply an occasional squirt of light oil (No. 10 engine oil thinned with kerosene) to the hole as the work progresses. This is adequate for most light jobs, although specific lubricants are better for heavy or prolonged drilling. (See Chapter 20, The Drill Press). The oil acts as a coolant to carry heat away from the bit. If the drill is running at a speed well above that recommended for the material being worked, it is also wise to remove the bit from the hole at frequent intervals to promote additional cooling. The result is longer bit life, less chance of drawing the drill's hardness.

In wood drilling with a twist drill bit it is often helpful to remove the bit

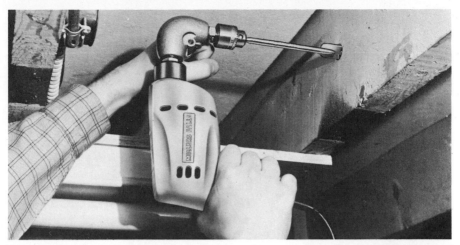

When work space is limited, right-angle drive takes over. Chuck is unscrewed from drill spindle and replaced by drive. Same chuck is then screwed onto output spindle of drive.

from the hole at least once or twice during the job if it is to penetrate deeply. Some woods tend to pack into the flutes of the drill bit, increasing friction, heating the bit, and in large diameters, increasing motor load. With the bit removed from the hole it is easy to remove the packed-in wood with a nail or awl. In some cases it is thrown out by centrifugal force if the drill is allowed to run free for a few seconds.

In all drilling of either wood or metal it is very important to avoid drill wobble, especially when using small-diameter bits. Here, the two-hand grip is your best bet aside from a drill-press attachment. A wobbling drill enlarges the hole and greatly increases the chance of bit breakage.

If a fixed-speed drill is to be used for a wide range of operations requiring extreme speed differences, use a power-tool speed regulator between the plug on the drill cord and the electrical outlet. Regulators of this type, such as those made by the Dremel Manufacturing Division, are suited to power drills up to 5 amp capacity. They provide variable speed simply by means of a control knob on the unit. For general workshop tasks, for example, you would use about 2000 r.p.m. to drill a $\frac{1}{16}''$ hole in plastic, 1200 r.p.m. for a $\frac{1}{4}''$ hole in wood, 1000 r.p.m. for a $\frac{3}{8}''$ hole in masonry (with a masonry bit), and about 700 r.p.m. to put a $\frac{1}{2}''$ hole in steel. The separate regulators can cover the zero to full-speed range the same as a variable-speed drill.

In working with any drill attachment keep in mind the fact that the drill's power is not equal to that of larger tools designed for the same job. A little experience will give you the feel of the drill with each accessory. The trick is in letting the tool drill or cut as fast as it can without forcing it.

Selecting a Power Drill. Aside from the basic factors of speed, power, and size, general quality is of major importance. Test the trigger switch action. It should be easy but positive. A hard-to-work trigger switch will be tiring to use. Let the drill run free and listen to it. The noise level varies from drill to drill but the sound should be free of any indication of gear chatter. With the drill stopped, hold the drill housing firmly in one hand and grip the chuck in the other. There should be little or no play in the bearing fit. As to the

For sharpening bits or other tools, grinder attachment replaces chuck. Mounting attachments directly on drill spindle rather than in chuck brings load closer to bearings, reduces wear.

bearings themselves, you'll find ball bearings in high-priced models, self-lubricating bronze in typical home shop models, often with a ball thrust bearing in the chuck spindle. Both types give excellent service if of good quality, and the difference in price of the drill is likely to be large. So for average use, this factor is not critical.

Ease of repair is another point to check. Look the drill over to determine how you replace a motor brush if necessary. Usually, an instruction book or manual is packed with the drill. If so, it will very likely give an indication of how this and similar minor jobs are done. In average shop work many drills operate for years without need for any repair whatever. But even the best tools can be damaged by accident. So it's wise to check on the availability of parts and the ease with which a damaged drill can be repaired. None involve much difficulty, though it's better to know the details in advance. In some types, brushes can be replaced by simply removing screw caps at the end of the drill housing. Others have a removable section of the housing. Many require the removal of the gear case at the front of the housing and general disassembly. A different and very convenient arrangement used in "clam shell" models utilizes a housing made in two lengthwise halves. Remove the assembly bolts, lift off one half, and you expose all internal parts like a cut-away drawing. Remove and replace any part, put the halves together, and the job's done.

CHAPTER FOURTEEN

THE SABRE SAW

THE SABRE SAW is one of the most versatile of portable power tools. It can make straight or curved cuts and it can make its own starting hole when a cut must begin in the middle of a board or panel. Many models are available with tilting shoe plates to permit bevel cutting. And most types can be adapted in seconds to cut metal or plastics as well as wood simply by changing blades.

A relatively new power tool, the portable sabre saw was a postwar development of Scintilla, S.A., a Swiss electrical manufacturer well known for aircraft magnetos. Today, most portable power-tool manufacturers include a sabre saw in their line.

The usual motor-driven sabre saw utilizes a planetary gear arrangement or a crank mechanism to transform the motor shaft rotation to reciprocal blade motion. In a typical model like the Stanley 90 454, the blade makes 3100 strokes

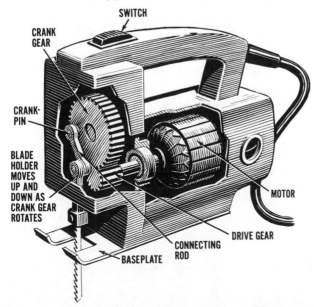

SWITCH

CRANK GEAR

CRANK-PIN

BLADE HOLDER MOVES UP AND DOWN AS CRANK GEAR ROTATES

MOTOR

DRIVE GEAR

CONNECTING ROD

BASEPLATE

How a sabre saw works: Drive gear from motor turns crank gear; crank pin converts rotary to vertical movement. Blade reciprocates at speeds ranging from 2000 to 10,000 strokes per minute, depending on model.

per minute. The teeth of the blade point upward so as to cut on the up stroke, which tends to hold the saw's shoe plate (the base on which it moves) firmly against the work. For cutting rubber, insulating wallboard, and similar materials, knife-edge blades without teeth are available. These cut on both up and down strokes, leaving no sawdust. When cutting some thermoplastics, however, the friction heat developed by any fast-moving blade tends to melt the plastic edges and fuse them together behind the blade as it passes through the work. To avoid this problem, a variable-speed saw may be used. Or a single-speed saw may be plugged into a speed-regulating unit like the Dremel regulator mentioned for power drills on page 91. Either way, the blade speed may be reduced to cut down friction heat. The simplest method of selecting the most suitable speed is by trial on a scrap of the material to be cut. Be sure, too, that the blade being used is suited to the material, as indicated on the opposite page.

There is another simple trick to eliminate it without turning the work over. Merely cover the outline to be cut with transparent cellulose tape, pressed down firmly. You can easily see the cutting line through it, but the tape holds the minute surface fibers in place as the blade passes upward through it on the cutting stroke. When the cut has been completed, peel off the slit tape.

Select a Sabre Saw according to the type of work it is to do. If you will be doing considerable on-the-spot cutting, as in making openings in wall paneling, cutting a window in a mounted door, or opening a ceiling for wiring changes, pick a lightweight saw. It will be easier to handle in awkward positions, especially overhead. If you must use the saw in cramped spaces, consider a model with a swiveling blade, like the Sears Scroller. This feature lets you lock the blade with the teeth sideways, frontward, or rearward for cutting in awkward spots. The blade may also be freed to turn in response to saw movement. It then swivels like a caster, bringing the toothed edge forward when the saw is moved in any direction.

Blades are made in a wide variety of general and special-purpose types, some manufacturers listing more than a dozen. The method of mounting the blade in the saw varies considerably with the make. On some, the upper end is notched to lock into the reciprocating rod. A setscrew inside the hollow rod is tightened from the top to provide a positive grip. Another type of blade is drilled through the upper end to take a small anchoring screw. A pin in the reciprocating rod provides two-point fastening. The simplest form, used by Stanley, Black & Decker, and many others, has a simple blank tip at the upper end of the blade. This fits into a slot in the reciprocating rod and is held firmly by a setscrew. An advantage of the blank tip blade lies in the fact that it is often possible to re-use it even after it breaks. As blade breakage usually occurs close to the upper end of the blade, you need only grind a short portion of the remaining blade section to remove the "set" of the teeth so the upper end will fit into the slot. The blade, though shorter, will still be usable on many jobs.

Blade teeth determine the type of cutting to which the blade is suited. Use

7-tooth, for fast, rough cuts in thick wood and plasterboard.

14-tooth, for soft, nonferrous metals (aluminum, copper, brass) up to ¼" thick.

7-tooth extra long, for sawing logs and timbers up to 4" thick. Usually 6" long.

24-tooth, for fine cuts in thin sheet metal and tubing, either ferrous or nonferrous.

10-tooth, for all-around use on hardwood, softwood, composition board, plastics.

32-tooth, for ferrous metals (iron and steel), pipe, and solid rod and bar stock.

10-tooth taper-ground, for fine cuts in plywood, veneer, plastic laminates.

Knife blade, for rubber, leather, wallboard, cloth, resilient floor tiles.

SELECT A BLADE TO FIT THE JOB

coarse teeth for fast work where absolute smoothness of the cut edge is not essential. For example, you'll save time in cutting a countertop sink opening by using a coarse blade. But if the countertop is covered with a plastic laminate you'll need finer teeth to avoid chipping. In general shop work you'll use coarse teeth more often than fine ones. But on cabinetwork, such as cutting a round or oval tabletop, favor the fine-toothed blade. It leaves a cut edge so smooth-surfaced that little or no sanding is necessary before finishing.

Metal-cutting blades must be selected to suit the thickness and type of metal to be cut. The basic principles are the same as with hand hacksaw blades, but the sabre-saw blade cannot be tilted like a hacksaw to prevent teeth from catching on the edge of thin sheet metal. To cut thin sheet metal pick the finest toothed blade and be sure the cutting line is firmly held. This can be managed by clamping a wood batten close to the line (if the line is straight) or by clamping the sheet metal between two layers of thin plywood if the cutting line is curved. Draw the outline to be cut on the upper surface of the plywood and cut through the metal and the two plywood layers in one operation. This eliminates the "chatter" that occurs when metal vibrates during cutting, a common cause of broken blade teeth. When cutting through tubing or irregular shapes use blocks of scrap wood to keep the saw level during the cut. If a tube rolls while being cut, blade breakage is likely. In most everyday metal cutting, however, no special set-up is necessary. The saw cut leaves a clean-cut edge without the waves that often result from shearing.

General Cutting Rules. In all sabre-saw work a few basic rules are important. First, when starting a cut from the edge of a board or panel, be sure the front of the saw's shoe plate is resting firmly on the surface of the work

To cut metal tubing, set it snugly between pieces of scrap wood, cut through both wood and tube. This prevents tube from rolling and possibly breaking blade.

When cutting thin sheet metal, clamp work between sheets of scrap plywood on which outline to be cut has been drawn. Plywood prevents metal from "chattering."

before the saw is started. The blade *should not* be in contact with the work at this stage. Start the saw and move the blade *gently* into the work. Pushing the blade into the work with a sudden bump is one of the commonest causes of blade breakage. You will quickly learn the forward speed at which your particular saw cuts most efficiently. A little experience in practice cutting is the best guide. In most cases the saw will be able to cut considerably faster than you will want to cut for the sake of accuracy in following the cutting outline. Do not "force" the saw. You won't gain any speed and may break a blade. But don't leave the blade running in the work with the saw at a standstill. Overheating the blade is likely to spoil it. When you remove the saw from the work *wait for the blade to stop.* If you lift the blade out of the work while it is still running, the tip is very likely to strike the wood surface, marring the work and possibly breaking the blade. Used properly, a wood-cutting blade should last for months of average workshop use. Many are still in use after years.

Curved Cuts. The sharper the curve the narrower the blade. That's the general rule in curve cutting. But for strength, sabre-saw blades have a minimum width seldom less than ¼". So don't expect to duplicate the extremely fine, small-radius work of the jigsaw or coping saw. To get the smallest radius cuts look for a narrow, hollow-ground blade with wide "set" to the teeth. This means that the teeth are bent outward to opposite sides to make a wide kerf in which the blade can turn more sharply. To get a visual picture of the radius cut you can expect from a blade make a short straight cut in scrap wood. Then, with the blade removed from the saw, insert it in the cut and turn it until its rear edge is snug against the side of the kerf. The angle it makes with the line of the cut is a fair indication of the turn it can take.

Ripping and Crosscutting. Most sabre-saw blades for woodwork are of a combination type suited to cutting either with or across the grain, as in curve cutting both directions are involved. When cutting through plywood or through several edge-joined boards it is best to grip the saw with both hands. The right hand can apply the forward pressure to the saw, the left hand can serve as a brake if needed. Watch for the saw to lurch forward suddenly as the blade cuts across the juncture between boards. A split-off section of wood

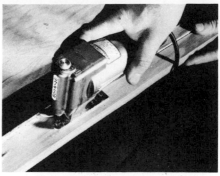

Squared crosscuts with sabre saw are easily made with a try square. Hold the shoe plate against the blade edge, which acts as a guide throughout the cut.

In ripping with sabre saw, clamp or nail a batten to the work as a guide. Some models can be fitted with an adjustable guide fence which grips edge of work.

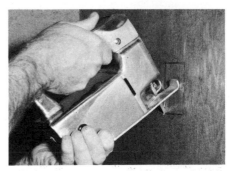

Plunge cuts in the middle of a panel are sabre saw's specialty. Clamp a batten at right angle across cutting line to serve as stop and pivot point for front of shoe plate.

Free-hand cut into wall paneling should be guided by both hands to prevent saw from veering as blade is tipped in.

on the underside may not be visible, but the lessened resistance will let the saw jump ahead. If it isn't held in check there's a chance of breaking the blade when it suddenly comes up hard again against the full wood thickness. In plywood, a "void" or gap in inner plies sometimes has the same effect. Keep these possibilities in mind and keep the saw moving steadily to get the most working life out of your blades.

Making a Starting Hole. The ability of the sabre saw to make its own starting hole in the center of a panel enables you to cut an opening for a cabinet door and use the cut-out section as the door. No edge will be marred by the notch left from a bored hole. The starting hole made by the saw is really a straight kerf, so it is a part of the overall cut. To make it, tip the saw forward so it rests on the front tips of the shoe plate with the blade tip just above the surface of the wood. The blade should be lined up exactly with the line to be cut, so that it will cut along that line as it is tipped back into the wood. You can aid accuracy by clamping a small batten across the line at right angles to it. If the tips of the shoe plate rest against this batten the saw will be parallel to the line. Start the saw with the blade just above the wood surface. Then *very gradually* tip it back so the blade tip contacts the wood. It will begin cutting at this point, so watch it carefully to be sure it is on the line. From here on, it is simply a matter of tipping the saw backward the rest of

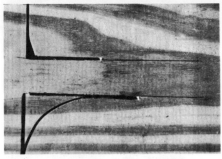

Two ways to turn a corner: Top, saw cut downward, then made series of angled shave cuts to provide room for blade to turn to right. Bottom, blade cut upward, then backed up and took curve cut to meet line to right. Saw was stopped, turned around, steered back along horizontal line to corner.

To cut a window opening in a hollow door, start from a bored hole (plunge cut may hit inner-core parts, cause breakage), then swing saw to outline.

the way as the blade cuts deeper into the wood. Once the blade emerges from the underside the saw can be gently seated on the work. To complete the cut merely remove the batten and continue along the line to the corner. Then stop the saw, lift it out, and cut back to the other corner. The same procedure is repeated on each side of a rectangular door cut. This procedure cannot be employed on a curved line.

Precision Hinging. When using a sabre saw in cabinet-door work in this way, you can assure accurate door hinging by a very simple trick. Cut three sides of the door opening, including the hinge side, leaving the fourth side uncut. Then mount the hinges on the hinge side. When this has been done make the cut for the fourth (latch) side. As the door was hinged before it was fully cut it will be perfectly aligned. It can then be removed for any further work such as attaching stop strips and catches.

Support the cut-out section in this and similar work, either by hand or by a piece of scrap wood clamped under the opening being cut. If the cut-out section is allowed to fall free it may tip to an angle and jam the blade as it falls. The support prevents this. The same precaution should be used when cutting an end off a heavy piece of wood.

Controlling Depth of Cut. This is another technique that widens the sabre saw's range of applications, allowing you to cut slots or designs in wood. Attach a wood shim of the proper thickness to the bottom of the shoe plate, raising the saw above the work so that the blade penetrates a lesser distance into the wood. The same effect is possible with a shorter blade, perhaps one that has been broken off and re-ground to fit in the attaching slot. With the depth of cut controlled by either of these methods, you must start the cut from the edge of the surface or from a hole bored in the center of the work. The shortened blade length will not permit the saw to be tilted into the wood, as in making a starting cut in door work. In all depth-controlled cutting one point is very important: the arrangement must never be such that the blade tip can rise completely above the wood surface on the up-stroke. The tip would then strike the surface on the down-stroke, resulting in breakage.

Bevel Cuts are a simple matter with sabre saws equipped with a tilting

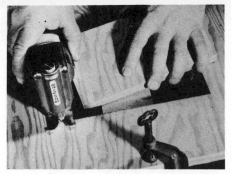

When cutting out section of a panel, clamp a batten under cut-out area so it won't tilt and jam blade, but can be lifted out.

To control depth of cut, fasten wood shims under shoe plate to prevent blade's full length from penetrating wood. Best method is to bolt shims on; if impossible, use double-coated, pressure-sensitive tape.

Samples of cuts that can be made with a sabre saw, for practical or artistic purposes, by controlling depth of blade.

Mortise cuts can be made with a sabre saw by using a short blade or shims under the shoe plate. First cut outline of mortise; then make series of short crosscuts so sections can be "clicked out."

shoe plate. But they can also be made with saws not so equipped. To cut a bevel with such a saw simply attach a wood shim strip to one side of the shoe plate to tilt it to the desired angle. If the tool is to be used for extensive bevel-cutting the shim may be attached with flathead bolts running up through

Bevel cuts along straight or curved lines are easily made if saw has tilting adjustment .

If saw lacks a bevel-cutting adjustment, scrap wood can be fastened to shoe plate to give necessary tilt.

Special guide for some model saws enables you to cut accurate circles. It can be adjusted to desired radius and screw-locked.

holes drilled in the shoe plate. On saws where this is not possible the shim may be attached with double-coated pressure-sensitive tape. This tape is adhesive-coated on both sides, with a peel-off protective strip on one side. Press it against the shoe plate with the peel-off strip out. Then peel off the strip to expose the adhesive surface, and press the wood against it. Provide as much contact area as possible.

Corner Cuts in everyday work may be made in two ways. In one, you cut along one side to the corner. Then back the saw about an inch away from the corner and make a curved cut leading to the adjoining side, and continue along that line to the opposite corner. Stop the saw, lift it out, and cut back to the first corner, severing the curved section left there. The other method calls for cutting to the corner, then backing the saw slightly. Then make a series of three or four short forward cuts, each veering a little more toward the adjoining line. When this procedure has produced a wedge-shaped opening large enough to turn the blade in, turn the saw to cut out along the adjoining line. Both basic cuts are shown in the photo of corner cuts.

Cutting Guides are available for some saws to make various cuts more accurate. Many modern saws, for example, may be used with a circle-cutting accessory that guides the saw around a center pin in a perfect circle. Adjust the circle arm to the desired radius and tighten it with a clamp screw before cutting. The same company makes an adjustable angle-cutting guide. The saw's special shoe plate rides a track at any pre-set angle. Many saws include an adjustable fence that can be set for ripping to any desired width.

CHAPTER FIFTEEN

THE PORTABLE CIRCULAR SAW

THE PORTABLE CIRCULAR SAW can do many of the operations of the table saw. It can crosscut, rip, miter, and bevel. Its depth of cut can be regulated so it can also do certain types of grooving, though the adjustment is seldom used for this purpose. More often, depth of cut is set to cut through one layer of· material without cutting into the layer behind or below it. If, for example, a section of finished floor must be removed without cutting the subfloor the saw can be adjusted to do the job.

Basically, this tool consists of a circular saw blade geared to a motor with a handle and trigger switch atop its housing. The upper portion of the blade is housed in a fixed guard. The lower portion projects downward through a flat base or shoe plate. The lower portion of the blade is covered by a movable guard that rotates backward around the saw spindle hub as it contacts the

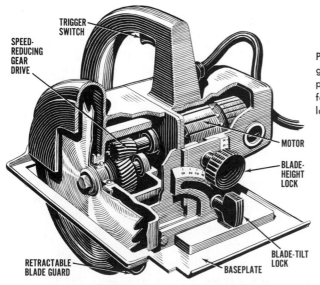

Portable circular saw with blade guard in safety position. Note protractor guide for tilting blade for bevel cuts, and blade-height lock for depth-of-cut adjustment.

wood being cut. As the saw progresses into the work, the guard rotates up-ward and out of the way inside the fixed upper guard housing. The saw blade rotates so that the teeth are traveling upward as they enter the work, thus tending to hold the saw down firmly on the surface. The tip of the spring-loaded movable lower guard rides along the surface of the work as the blade passes through it. As the saw completes the cut and moves out of the far side, the lower guard swings downward again and covers the lower portion of the blade. The guard is important for protecting the operator even after a cut is completed, as most saws of this type continue to "coast" for a period after they are shut off.

Picking the Right Saw. For a given blade size, the portable saw is usually more powerful than a table saw (typically 1 to 2 h.p.) in order to provide reserve power for cutting heavy (and often damp) lumber on building jobs. Models are available with blades from 5½″ to more than 8″. Most of the 5½″ and 6″ units will cut through a 2-by-4 at 90 degrees, but you need a 6½″ blade size to cut the same lumber at 45 degrees, a type of cut frequently required in building work. So, if you have major remodeling in mind, select a saw with at least a 6½″ blade, or 7″ for a little extra margin. The difference in price is not likely to be large. The smaller saws, being lighter in weight, are often used by builders as a "second saw" for use in awkward positions and on thinner stock like flooring and sheathing. They can also handle the usual square cuts through nominal 2″ stock.

Among the features that add to the usefulness of these tools are such items as a rip guide. This is an adjustable-length arm that can be extended outward from the side of the saw base to serve as a rip fence does on a table saw. It is locked in position by a clamping knob. A graduated protractor on the bevel adjustment is another convenience. An important point to look for is an ample-sized retracting lever on the movable blade guard. This should be easy to reach and operate, as there are various types of work on which the guard must be lifted out of the way before the saw goes into action. (More about this later.) Be sure, too, that the depth-of-cut adjustment has a knob or wing nut of sufficient size to make it easy to clamp it firmly in position.

Blades. The portable saw uses the same blade types as the table saw, but it is not designed for use with such special accessories as dado heads or mold-ing cutters. It is a good tool for use with abrasive cut-off wheels, however. Though its blade housing and guard are seldom as heavy as those on regular cut-off machines using wheels of this type, they offer better protection for this kind of work than is found on most table saws. As with a table saw, the handiest blade is a combination type. For average use it is wise to keep an extra blade on hand to use while the other one is being sharpened. Many workers select a finer toothed combination blade for the spare, as the two types can do the same jobs and offer a choice of fast cutting or slightly slower cutting with a smoother finish. (For descriptions of a wider range of blade types see Chapter 18, The Table Saw.)

Operation. Perhaps the most important single factor in using this type of saw is a firm grip. A typical 6½″ model weighs around 11 or 12 pounds. Rest the front of the saw base, or shoe plate, on the work before starting the saw,

Correct grip on saw and work for cross-cutting along pencil line. Blade guard is being pushed inside upper blade housing. Note that cutting guide on front of saw base lines up exactly with blade.

Rip guide, graduated in inches for easy setting, assures straight cut. Knob clamps it at chosen width.

but do not have the blade in contact with the wood. The blade teeth can hook into the wood and stall the saw unless the saw is in motion before contact is made. Line up the blade with the cutting line before you pull the trigger switch. All saws of this type provide a slot or other guide at the front of the shoe plate to serve as a guide to the blade position slightly farther back. If you are cutting material appreciably thinner than the saw's capacity you can reduce friction, as on a table saw, by adjusting the depth of cut so the blade will protrude only about ¼″ through the work. Once the saw is started move it steadily through the work. Be sure the work is not supported in such a way as to cause binding as the saw progresses. For example, avoid cutting in a manner that would cause the work to pinch inward against the blade. If the blade should happen to bind, shut off the saw immediately, find the cause of trouble, and correct it. Then complete the cut. As the saw emerges from the work on the far side be prepared to support its weight. You are pushing the saw as it cuts but you must hold it up after cut-off. The knack comes quickly, but it is best to make your first few cuts in a comfortable position with a firm stance, and use scrap wood for the purpose. The firm stance is always an essential, but with experience, you will be less concerned about the comfortable aspect of the job.

This lightweight saw makes 45-degree angle cut through 2-by-4. Smaller saws can cut through at 90 degrees but not at 45.

Pocket cut requires deft saw handling. Saw is tilted upward on front of base, then lowered into work. Guard must be retracted by pulling lever up and forward.

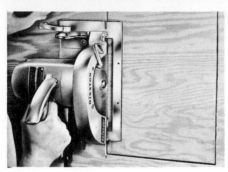

Square or rectangular openings may be cut in panel materials by easing blade down into material in pocket-cut fashion. No starting-kerf with hand saw need be made if done properly.

Saw blade is not deflected by angled entry into work, as in trimming ends of diagonal flooring. When saw must enter wood at longer angle, guard is retracted to prevent its jamming against work.

Long cuts through panel materials too wide for the use of the rip guide are best made with the saw riding against a batten clamped or temporarily nailed in place as a guide. This assures a straight cut even though you may have to change positions several times during the cut, in order to maintain your grip on the saw. It is important in this kind of work, too, that the cut-off section be well supported. If it is not, its weight will tend to jam the blade during the cut; near the finish, the small section of uncut material remaining may break.

Long ripping jobs through damp or pitchy wood will not be slowed if the cut is wedged slightly open after the saw has progressed a few feet. A small wooden wedge driven lightly into the starting end of the cut will do the job. If a wedge isn't on hand you can drive a nail into the cut near the end. The nail diameter should be a little greater than the natural width of the cut.

Crosscutting is extremely simple and fast in most cases, though it pays to make a few practice cuts in scrap material to get the feel of the saw before you tackle your first piece of work. Some saws tend to follow a straight line with almost no steering effort on the part of the operator. Others require a little hand pressure in one direction or the other. Sometimes re-positioning your hand on the handle does the trick.

Pocket cuts. These are the cuts that call for tipping the saw upward at the rear with the front of its base, or shoe plate, resting on the work. The movable guard is tilted out of the way by means of the lever provided for the purpose. Then the saw is started and tilted gradually down again so the blade cuts downward into the work from above. This is a technique used to start a cut in the mid-area of a panel or to remove a section from the edge of a piece of lumber after end cuts have been made inward from the edge. This is definitely not a trick for the beginner, but a useful one later on. The blade must be lowered into the wood gently but with a very firm grip. Keep in mind that the blade is like a wheel spinning backward at around 6500 r.p.m (no load) and trying to drive the saw backward. Properly handled, the blade cuts into the wood easily and with surprisingly little back thrust. But rack up some experience on regular cutting before you try pocket cuts.

Masonry cutting requires a reinforced abrasive cut-off wheel in place of

Marble and other hard stone can be cut in stages with masonry wheel, taking cut of about 3/16" depth to start, increasing depth by same amount with each pass.

the saw blade. This type of wheel is reinforced by nylon, cloth, or glass fiber pressed into the resin that bonds the abrasive together. An abrasive wheel must be used with care, however, as it breaks much more easily than a metal blade—which in normal use is practically unbreakable.

A major factor in this type of work is an unwavering cut. Any veering flexes the abrasive wheel and invites breakage. An experienced operator cutting relatively soft materials such as cement block can make the relatively short cuts freehand. But harder materials such as marble require the use of a guide batten clamped firmly to the work so the saw base can slide along it. In hard materials of this type the saw is set for a depth of cut not greater than $3/16''$. After each pass, the depth is increased by the same amount until the material is severed. But the job is still a fast one. To cut a 1" thick piece of marble 12" wide takes less than a minute.

Metal cutting is done with a similar type of wheel. But be sure the wheel you are using is made specifically for the type of material being cut. *Do not* use a masonry wheel on metal or vice versa, and buy your wheel according to the kind of metal to be cut. The maximum speed at which any abrasive wheel can safely operate is always printed on it or on the paper disks called "blotters" stuck to its sides. *Never* run the wheel faster than this speed, and preferably well under it. In general, this type of wheel is rated well within the speed of the average saw. But check the speed on the saw's specification plate to make sure.

CHAPTER SIXTEEN

POWER SANDERS

POWER SANDERS make finishing easier and faster. Misplace a single pencil line across a foot of dressed pine and you'll spend at least five minutes hand-sanding to remove it. But practically any power sander can do the job inside of thirty seconds. Depending on its form it can also do other things, such as carving, beveling, trimming, and mitering wood. Some can even shine your shoes or polish your silver—with felt or flannel in place of the abrasive.

You can take your pick from basic workshop types that range from a power-drill attachment that spins at 2500 r.p.m. to an orbital unit that makes better than 11,000 strokes a minute, or a belt job that sands at 20 feet a second. In between, you can choose from an array of orbitals, reciprocals, drums, and disks to handle any form of sanding you'll ever encounter. Each has some distinct tricks of its own, and sometimes a drawback or two. Knowing these traits is your best guide to sander selection in your work.

A few general rules apply. Use either rotary or straight-line sanders for rough and intermediate sanding, for unstained natural finishes and for paint. But for top-quality stained finishing use only straight-line sanding with the grain. (If the only sander available is a rotary sander you can hand-sand the

Tilt flexible disc so only outer third touches work, minimizing swirl marks. One-hand grip helps you apply smooth, even pressure through a flexible wrist motion.

final stage.) Stain emphasizes sanding marks that are all but invisible on the bare wood beforehand. If they run with the grain they are camouflaged and inconspicuous. If they run in circles they tell the world you used the wrong sander. As to sander speed, the faster the abrasive moves over the surface the cleaner its shearing action. Slow movement tends to pull and tear fibers, leaving a rougher surface.

To get a sander that suits your type of work, weigh these facts:

Flexible Disk Attachments for power drills will take any abrasive paper grade, and they cut fast. At 2400 r.p.m. coarse aluminum oxide on a 5" disk can chew the corners off a pine 1-by-2 to make a 45-degree picket point in seventy seconds. It's tops for dressing up rough surfaces, removing material, skinning off heavy paint, and for shaping jobs such as rounding and contouring model boat hulls. But for finish sanding without circular scratches, digs and ripples, it requires more handling skill than any other type—skill you may not have.

For the best chance, hold it tipped not more than 15 degrees to flex the outer third of the disk against the wood and get the advantage of the high rim speed, 3000 feet per minute at 2400 r.p.m. Hold it so the working edge of the rim is traveling with the grain and keep the sander moving grainwise along the wood. On each pass let the outer portion of the rim overlap about half an inch on to the area previously sanded by the slower-moving inner portion, to level the surface. Keep pressure light and don't pause. Held in one spot for just ten seconds with coarse paper, the disk will cut a ¼" deep crescent in pine. Don't start with a coarser abrasive than the surface requires and don't skip more than one grit size as you shift to finer paper. With fine finishing paper the disk clears pine of a pencil line equal to its diameter in ten seconds sanding with the grain, four seconds across it. Don't use it on spackled wallboard seams. Any paper coarse enough not to clog will cut too fast for safe control.

Ball joint disc won't dig in even if the drill is tilted. Ball joint allows drill to tilt while disc stays flat on surface.

Rigid disc on a table saw cuts bevels almost as fast as a router, more smoothly than a saw. This one is homemade 8" disc cut from ¾" plywood.

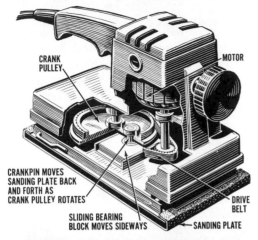

CRANK
PULLEY

MOTOR

CRANKPIN MOVES
SANDING PLATE BACK
AND FORTH AS
CRANK PULLEY ROTATES

DRIVE
BELT

SLIDING BEARING
BLOCK MOVES SIDEWAYS

SANDING PLATE

Finishing sanders have either a reciprocating or an orbital action. They are designed for fine smoothing jobs on work to be stained.

To level the bumps in a spackled seam, a vibrating sander is a good choice. It takes down the bumps but spares the paper.

The Ball Joint Disk (Swirlaway) is rigid, rubber-cushioned, with its shaft on a universal joint, so tipping the power drill won't vary the pressure across its face. As it is only 4″ in diameter, and only 1¼″ of the disk contacts the surface, there isn't much speed differential over the working area. The paper-gripping hub is recessed so the disk can be used flat on the work. Keep it moving and overlap successive passes slightly, using light pressure to keep r.p.m. up. Good for general preliminary sanding, it's especially suited to wavy surfaces such as old paneling and furniture. It rides over and adapts to the contours, smoothing without "sanding through" stain or patina of high spots. Used carefully, it can smooth wallboard seams. It cuts through paper surfacing in seven seconds. It's not for carving or heavy-material removal, but is a good general cabinet sander for the small shop, much easier to use than the flexible disk with its tendency to scratch and dig.

Rigid Disk Sanders (sanding plates) fit your table saw arbor, though you'll do better with a double-sided homemade plywood one. (Coarse abrasive on one side, fine on the other speeds the work.) An 8″ disk at 3000 r.p.m. has a rim speed well over a mile a minute, fast enough to do trimming, beveling, and related work almost as fast as a jointer, and fast enough to require goggles for chip and abrasive throw-off protection. Take successive light cuts as attempts to take heavy ones will loosen and tear the abrasive paper.

Orbital sander is especially suited to working into corners. It is also effective for smoothing miter joints.

Reciprocating Sanders, also called stroke sanders, impart a straight back-and-forth motion to the abrasive paper at speeds of 4000 strokes per minute or more. As the tool may be positioned to sand with the grain of the wood it is widely used in finishing cabinetwork. Where considerable material must be removed, the sander may be applied across the grain for faster, but rougher, cutting. Final smoothing may then be done with the grain. The sander may also be tipped at an angle over the edge of a board to round off sharp corners, as on square-edged lumber. For this, the motion should be parallel to the grain. To avoid overrounding, it's wise to try this procedure first on scrap wood to learn the cutting speed of your particular sander. In all sanding work, keep the sander moving along over the work. If it is allowed to remain in one place it cuts more deeply into that area, resulting in an uneven surface or edge. Some higher priced sanders of this type are "dual action" forms that can be converted from reciprocating action to orbital action (described next) merely by moving a lever. This feature provides the advantages of two sanders in one, and lets you select the type of sanding motion that best suits the job.

Orbital Sanders, instead of moving the abrasive back and forth, give it a small-diameter rotary motion. It doesn't spin like a disk sander, but moves in an orbit that combines forward and sideward motion so that each grain on the abrasive surface travels in a small circle, typically of about ⅛″ to ³⁄₁₆″ diameter, at rates as high as 11,000 orbits per minute. Because of the small-diameter movement and high speed, the abrasive doesn't leave swirl marks. An advantage of the orbital sander: it can produce an even finish on areas where the grain runs in several directions, as at a miter or butt joint, where straight-line motion would result in cross-sanding one part. (The effect of different sanding motions on work to be stained is explained in Chapter 11.)

Drum (or spindle) **sanders** are sold in assorted sizes, usually in kits of about five. Major abrasive manufacturers make the replacement sleeves to fit them, commonly ranging in diameter from ½″ to 2″. These are strictly

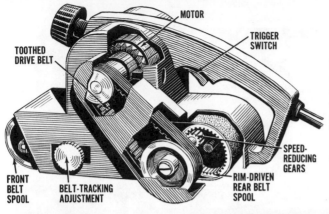

MOTOR

TRIGGER
SWITCH

TOOTHED
DRIVE BELT

SPEED-
REDUCING
GEARS

FRONT
BELT
SPOOL

BELT-TRACKING
ADJUSTMENT

RIM-DRIVEN
REAR BELT
SPOOL

Belt sander is built for rough work. Two spools, one on each end of the tool, are fitted with a removable abrasive belt. The rear spool is powered by motor through a reduction drive.

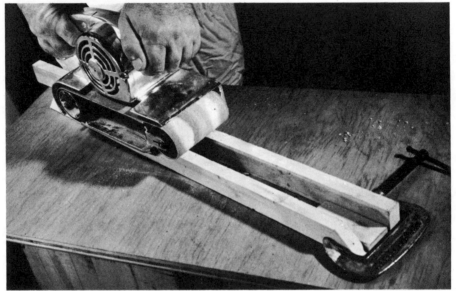

When sanding narrow stock with the belt sander, clamp a second strip in place to hold the sander level, insure a square edge.

special-purpose tools for use on narrow concave edges as in scroll-cut work, but if you do the cutting with a fine blade at high speed you may not need a sanding job at all. A few smaller sizes are handy, however, for enlarging and edge-smoothing bored or drum-sawed holes. In use, move the drum sander *against* the direction of the drum rotation. Moving it with the rotation direction can cause it to "kick" into faster motion, resulting in momentary loss of control and damage to the work.

The Belt Sander is geared for big jobs such as boats, interior trim and major-sized cabinet work. It cuts fast with coarse abrasive for rough material removal, and with a fine belt does quality final-stage finish-sanding with the grain. Its straight-line belt travel suits both jobs. On cupped boards, move the sander along at 45 degrees to the grain so the working surface of the belt rides on the high edges of the board, cutting them down. Usually one pass in each direction plus a final one with the belt running with the grain, will give

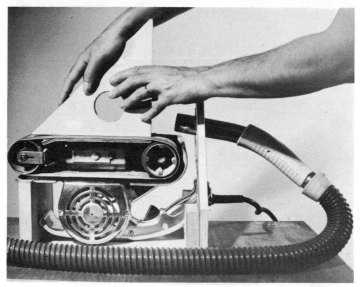

Homemade stand converts a portable belt sander into a bench tool. The bracket holds vacuum-cleaner hose near work to suck up the dust.

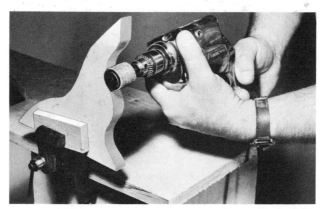

Sanding drums up to 3″ in diameter, used with a power drill, do a fast job of smoothing and shaping contour surfaces.

the required flat surface—useful trick in cabinetwork. For top-speed rough-cutting it can be used directly across the grain, but split-out fibers at the rear may result.

Despite its cutting speed the belt sander may seem slow if you are watching a blemish on a low area of the wood, as the steel platen that backs the working area of the belt causes the sander to cut down high spots and level a surface before reaching the low spots. (Rubber-cushioned sanders like rotaries, vibrators, and orbitals adapt to minor surface contours but don't do a full leveling job.)

Treat the belt sander's trigger lock with respect, and with it fixed in the "on" position never let go of the sander. A 14-pounder can take off across the floor at almost 20 miles an hour, faster than you can run, and fast enough to smash furniture, walls, or to sail off a stair well or boat deck.

CHAPTER SEVENTEEN

THE ROUTER

THE ROUTER is a useful tool in general woodworking and an almost indispensable tool in cabinet work. Basically, it consists of a high-speed motor mounted in vertical-shaft position on a flat base. A collet-type chuck on the lower end of the shaft permits the attaching of router bits in an almost limitless variety of shapes. The entire motor and shaft unit may be raised or lowered to regulate the distance the router bit projects below the base.

To visualize the operating principle of the router, suppose a perfectly circular router bit about the size of a dime is attached to the shaft end. If the router is now set down with its base on the surface of a board and the dime-shaped bit alongside the board edge you are ready to work. Start the router, move the dime-shaped cutter into the board edge, then along it. The result will be a rounded groove along the board edge, with a curvature matching the perimeter of the cutter. With more elaborately shaped cutters you can

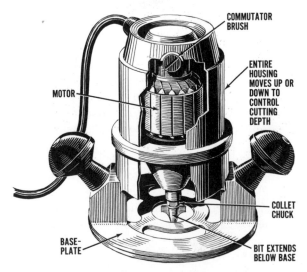

COMMUTATOR BRUSH

ENTIRE HOUSING MOVES UP OR DOWN TO CONTROL CUTTING DEPTH

MOTOR

COLLET CHUCK

BASE-PLATE

BIT EXTENDS BELOW BASE

Basic parts of simple router. Depth-of-cut adjustment is usually by screw thread with locking clamp. Guides attach to fittings on base.

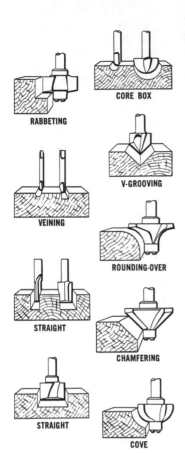

RABBETING

CORE BOX

V-GROOVING

VEINING

ROUNDING-OVER

STRAIGHT

CHAMFERING

STRAIGHT

COVE

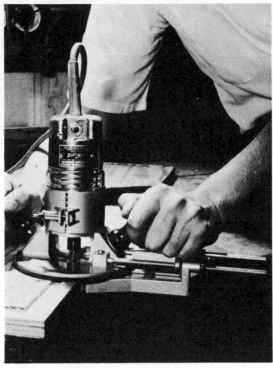

Grooving a plywood panel with the straightedge guide. Threaded adjusting rod places bit at desired distance from the panel edge.

Some of the many cuts possible with a router. Different types of cutters may be used successively in parallel passes to produce elaborate moldings.

cut any desired form of molding in board or panel edges. Actually, this type of work is not done freehand. A guide is attached to the router base. This is adjusted so that it slides along the board or panel edge, holding the router with its shaft and bit at the correct distance from the edge for the proper depth of cut.

But the router is not limited to edge work. It also can cut an almost endless variety of grooves and recesses in the surface of a board or panel. With the standard guides it can cut the recesses for door and cabinet hinges to exact depth and shape, cut both mortises and tenons, form all parts of a dovetail joint or a box joint. And that is only a small part of its range of operations. It can make the precision cuts required in inlay work, cut the fluting in decorative furniture legs and follow templates to cut almost any design into the wood surface. With experience you can write your name in the form of a groove in the wood surface, using a small bit called a veining bit.

Router Guides vary in detail with the make, but certain forms are available for most routers. Most important is the guide for straight and circular cutting. This is usually attached by rods matched to fittings on the router base. The guide itself may be slid inward or outward along the rods and clamped

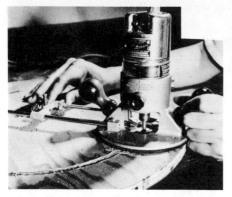

Routing a perfect circle. A trammel point, mounted on adjustable guide rods, is inserted in wood surface to act as compass point. Router then moves in perfect circle.

Plywood template is used to cut hardboard to same shape. Template guide, attached to base of router, prevents blade from cutting template while it cuts the work.

so as to hold the router bit at the desired distance from the edge of the work. Many types have a vernier adjustment for precision work. When used along straight edges the guide is fitted with a straight-sliding contact plate. When used to follow curved edges the straight-slide plate is removed and contact is through two rounded points. For making perfect circular cuts a trammel point is available for most of these guides. This is adjusted to the radius of the circle desired, setting the space between the point and the bit. Then, with the point held in the surface of the work (like the point of a drawing compass) the router is moved around it, cutting a perfectly circular groove.

Another very useful guide, especially in decorative work, is the template guide. This is in the form of a circular metal plate that attaches to the router base. A metal collar projects downward from the center of the plate surrounding the shank of the router bit. This collar prevents the bit from touching the template, which is clamped or nailed on top of the work to be cut. But it allows the lower portion of the bit to cut the work below the template as the collar slides along the outline.

To make the template first sketch the desired design on paper. Then transfer it to hardboard or ¼" plywood with carbon paper. Clamp the template material on the workbench with scrap wood under it. Adjust the router so the bit will cut about $\frac{1}{16}$" deeper than the thickness of the template material, and use it to cut out the template freehand, following the carbon-paper outline. Any errors in the template can be filed off or filled in with plastic wood before the template is used to rout the actual work. In doing the final work, itself, the router may be adjusted to reproduce the template design with a groove or recess in the work or by cutting all the way through. If all material is to be routed to a fixed depth inside the outline, the router is simply run repeatedly across the area, using a large bit to remove the material. It cannot break through the outline so long as the template remains in place. Removing material in this way is necessary when turning out such projects as partitioned wooden trays.

Shaper Conversion. Many routers can be converted to use as a shaper by mounting them upside down with the shaft end projecting upward through a table. A guide fence is used to assure a straight run of stock through the cutter. Such a conversion table unit is available for the Millers Falls Dyno-Mite router shown in the photos, and for Stanley routers and others. By tilting the router in the Stanley unit, more than 600 different molding forms can be produced with combinations of only four different shaper cutters.

Operating Technique. Most router shafts turn in a clockwise direction when viewed from above, as you look down on the router in working position. In all work where the bit is cutting along an edge the router must move in such a direction that motion of the router is against the rotation of the bit. This means that the router must move in a counterclockwise direction when cutting a molding edge on a circular tabletop (or oval). When cutting a molding along a straight edge the router should move from left to right, as viewed from the operator's position.

The speed of feeding the router through the work depends on the size of the cut and the hardness of the wood being worked. This calls for the development of "feel" in using the tool. The sound of the motor is one good guide. Turning free, some routers (such as the one in the photos) turn as fast as 30,000 r.p.m. As the bit enters the wood the motor slows down. The router should not be moved so fast through the work that the motor labors. At proper feed speed the motor will be somewhat slowed from its normal r.p.m., but it should have the general sound of running free. At the right rate the bit will cut easily and smoothly. Do not be too timid about the subject, however, and feed the work too slowly. If the bit lingers and does not move along steadily it is likely to overheat enough to draw the temper. A little experience (often during the first tryout) gives the average user the feel of the tool.

In all work hold the router firmly on the work. Keep a good grip on it

Chamfering with a router. When chamfer, bevel, or other cut is not to run entire length of an edge, router is stopped and backed off, leaving end of cut smoothly contoured (foreground).

Cutting a dado with router and straight-edge guide. When dado is located far from board end, a wooden batten is clamped across board to guide router.

particularly in starting, as the sudden torque of the high-speed motor tends to twist the tool in your hands as it accelerates. As with all power tools, keep your hands and fingers away from revolving cutters and bits. And never attempt to change bits or cutters or make adjustments without *disconnecting* the motor. Shutting it off at the switch on the tool is not enough. An accidental bump against the switch can start the motor all too easily.

Grooves and Dadoes. Though these cuts look alike, the dado is technically a cut made *across* the grain while a groove or plow cut is made *with* the grain. As the dado may be made across a board far from either end (as in dadoing uprights to take bookshelf ends) it is seldom possible to use one of the standard readymade router guides. The best guide for the job is a straight-edged piece of wood clamped to the work so as to guide the bit along the line to be cut. To place the wood guide properly measure the distance from the cutting edge of the bit to the outside edge of the router base. This is the distance the wood guide should be from the nearest edge of the dado.

Groove cutting is usually a simple matter of setting the readymade guide on the router, as with-the-grain cuts are seldom so far from the board edge that this type of guide will not span the distance.

The rabbet is simply a groove cut in the edge of a board or panel (either with or across the grain) so as to remove one corner. The result is a "step" in the edge. As this type of cut, by definition, is always made in the edge of the work the standard guide may be used. When an extremely wide rabbet must be cut, however, as in making a lap joint, the cut may have to be made in several passes.

Selecting Bits. Choose the bit that suits the job best. If you have a wide groove to cut favor a wide bit. (Users sometimes lazily use the bit that happens to be in the chuck.) You can, of course, use a narrow bit in several passes, but it means twice the working time and more bit wear. To get the best results with the least effort and tool wear familiarize yourself with the various bits available for your router. For all makes the selection is wide.

Where the utmost precision is important, as in matching the edges of a drop-leaf table joint, make trial cuts in scrap material. Fit the parts together for checking. In this type of work go all the way and fit the hinges to the scrap with a few screws so you can test the action. A cove bit makes the cut on the table leaf, a rounding-over bit of matching radius makes the cut in the tabletop. But both must be set properly to mate.

The following are some of the more common router bits available:

Ogee Bits. For making decorative cuts. Clamp straight edge or template on the work and use as a guide for the outside edge of router base.

Straight Deep Cutting Bit. For making successively deeper cuts in design work. The shank of the bit serves as a guide after the first cut is made.

Bits for Hinge Mortising. Fast cutting bits for mortising when cut is started from the edge of the work.

Long-Shank Straight Bits. Used for general purpose routing where depth of cut demands longer shank extension.

"V" Grooving Bits. For lettering and sign work.

Straight Double End Bits. Used for intricate line designs.

Straight Bits. These are used for all general purpose routing such as dado-ing, grooving, rabbeting.

Shear-Cut Bits. Those with a down-cutting action are fine for grooving veneered work as they produce very fine edges. Those with an up-cutting action lift chips out of the groove so deep cuts can be made.

Veining Double-End and Single-End Bits. For decorative thin-line work on any flat surface.

Core Box Bits. Fine for fluting flat surfaces.

Rabbeting Bits. These are commonly equipped with a pilot for rabbeting without using the router guide.

Stair Routing Bits. Used for grooving stair stringers for setting in steps and risers.

Combination Panel and Pilot-Panel Bits. Used for template panel routing and trimming veneer.

Straight Bits. For general-purpose routing.

Metal-Cutting Straight Bits. For cutting soft metals such as lead or zinc.

Dovetail Bits. Used to make dovetail joints.

Chamfering Bits. For decorative edgings and concealed joints.

Rounding Over and Cove Bits. For decorative edging and joints as in drop-leaf tables.

Beading and Roman Ogee Bits. For decorating furniture of various periods. Pilot is used to guide the router along the edge of the work.

CHAPTER EIGHTEEN

THE TABLE SAW

THE TABLE SAW is the kingpin of the average power-tool workshop. It can rip, crosscut, miter, and bevel. And it not only does it many times faster than a hand saw, but more accurately. Because it can be pre-set for precision cutting to widths and angles, it enables the average do-it-yourselfer to duplicate the accuracy of the master craftsman.

But sawing is only part of the table saw's range of operations. It can cut grooves of all types, and with a molding head in place of the saw blade it can produce almost any form of molding. With a sanding disk in place of the blade it can do power sanding rapidly enough to pinch hit for a planer on many jobs.

Basically, the table saw is simply a table with a slot in it through which the upper portion of a circular saw blade protrudes. The blade rotates toward

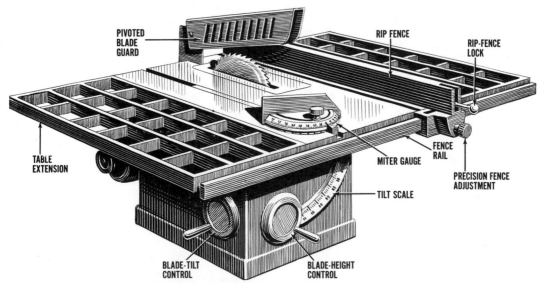

Basic parts of the table saw. Smaller models may lack precision fence adjustment or table extensions, but a little extra care or ingenuity can make up for missing refinements.

Extra-length keyed miter gauge allows you to cut large panels. Sliding portion of gauge is grooved to match key in side of slot in saw table. Gauge won't tip up or fall out when extended well beyond table edge.

the front of the table (where the operator stands) so the teeth travel downwards where the wood enters the saw. This tends to press the work down against the table.

With the exception of extremely elemental types, all saw tables have two guides to steer the work through the saw along a pre-set path. One is the "fence." This is a flat-surfaced metal bar that always remains parallel to the blade, though it can be slid toward or away from the blade and locked at any desired distance from it. This controls the width of the piece being cut. If you want to rip an 8″ board to 4″ width simply lock the fence in position 4″ from the blade, keep the work firmly against the fence as you push it through the saw, and you have a board 4″ wide.

The other guide is the "miter gauge." This slides in a groove parallel to the saw blade but its upper portion (the part that seats against the wood being worked) can be adjusted to any angle and locked. Lock it at 45 degrees, hold a piece of wood against it as you slide the miter gauge past the blade, and the wood will be cut at 45 degrees.

Safety Features. Most table saws are fitted with a removable saw guard that covers the exposed portion of the blade. This is a light metal housing with the front end sloped upward like a sled runner, and the rear end pivoted behind the blade. When a board is pushed toward the blade it first contacts the sloping front of the guard, lifting it so the board can slide under it and into the blade. But the guard still covers the portion of the blade protruding through the wood, preventing the operator's hands from contacting it by accident or carelessness. The guard should be used whenever possible. But it must be removed for many types of work. For example, when the work is higher than the pivot of the guard it could not pass under the guard and would be blocked. So the guard must be removed.

The "splitter" is another feature that contributes both to safety and sawing efficiency. This is a removable metal plate that projects upward behind the blade and directly in line with it. (The guard is often pivoted from the top of the splitter.) The splitter has several purposes. For one, it holds the saw cut open and prevents the wood from pinching inward against the rear of the blade. This type of binding can throw the work upward and forward toward the operator. The splitter also acts as a sort of rudder, assuring a straight-line

Blade guard protects operator's hands as he guides work into saw. Here the guard has ridden up on work, which slides beneath it to complete the cut.

cut. Pivoted from one side of the splitter are the "anti-kickback fingers." These are flat metal plates of graduated lengths with their lower ends serrated. Because of their varied lengths one of these metal fingers is always near vertical position when the others have been tilted up by the wood passing under them. If, by any chance, the wood is kicked forward due to binding against the blade the near-vertical anti-kickback finger will jam it down against the table with a cam action, stopping the kickback. The finger releases as the wood is again pushed forward.

When working with well-seasoned non-pitchy wood, binding and kickback are not apt to occur. But a dull blade or one with insufficient set can still cause the same effect. So on ripping work it's wise to utilize the splitter and anti-kickback fingers.

If you see a fellow shop worker using his saw without the guard on work where a guard could be used, it is probably because he learned to use a saw that way and now regards the guard as an inconvenience. So, if you're a beginner, learn to work with the guard from the start. It does not interfere with most work or with accuracy. The blade is plainly visible either through an opening in the guard top or through a plastic window. Why some workers don't use it: many early model saws were sold without a guard, supplying it as an extra accessory.

General Safety Pointers. Always maintain the utmost respect for the saw blade. Never push work into the saw in such a manner that a sudden slip could send your hands into the blade. This means that narrow work should be pushed, not by hand, but by a push stick. This is a stick of scrap wood long enough to keep hands well clear of the blade. The business end is notched to fit over the upper rear corner of the work. When a very small piece must be run through the saw use a length of scrap wood to hold it down also. In short, never take a risky grip with your fingers. Let push sticks of scrap wood do the job.

When work is being pushed through the saw by hand, as in everyday crosscutting, hold on to the supported piece (the piece pushed by the miter gauge) *only*. Never hold on to the free, cut-off piece, or pick it up with the saw running. Most crosscutting can be done with one hand. Holding on to the free piece with the other hand can't help and may cause the kerf to bind against the blade, causing a kickback that can bounce your hand into the blade.

In sawing, as in most power-tool work, one other precaution is essential. Don't wear loose, dangling clothing, such as half-rolled sleeves or a swinging necktie. They can be hooked by a saw tooth as easily as by a spinning piece of lathe work.

Ripping requires that the fence be exactly parallel to the blade. If the fence is off angle with its back end closer to the blade than the front, the work will bind and scorch the side of the kerf nearest the fence. If the fence is off angle in the opposite way, with the far end farther from the blade, the work will tend to creep away from the fence and the cut is apt to run on a taper. So follow the instructions for checking and adjusting the fence that come with your particular saw. You can check by measuring between the front edge of the blade and the fence, then the back edge. Use a combination square with its handle seated against the fence, its blade extended to measure distance to the saw blade. The method of adjustment depends on the make of saw. Once the fence is aligned it will remain that way unless roughly handled.

Start the cut with the fence set to the width desired. If you are in doubt make a trial cut in scrap wood and measure the width. Then re-set the fence if necessary. This is a good idea in fine work as different blades make kerfs of different widths, depending on thickness of blade and blade set. If the board is a long one stand in a comfortable position behind the saw and, using both hands, move the work into it along the fence. When most of the board has passed through the saw a safe way to finish is by the "pull-through" method. Simply walk around to the back of the saw and pull the remainder of the board through the saw. This way your hands are never near the blade, especially at the finish when the extended board end may tend to bounce or see-saw over the end of the table. The splitter is a help in this method as it keeps the board aligned while you walk around the saw.

Short pieces may be pushed all the way through by hand if the piece between the blade and the fence (the piece you will be pushing) is 3″ or more in width. If it is narrower use a push stick—or play ultra safe and use it anyway.

Beveling is simply a matter of tilting the blade or table to the desired angle, locking it, and proceeding as in square-edge cutting. On a tilting table saw the fence should be set on the low side of the table, below the blade. This way, it supports the work, and on narrow work, is in no danger of contacting the blade. On a tilt-arbor saw place the fence in the same relative position. In crosscut beveling the miter gauge is set in the table groove below the blade (or same relative position on tilt-arbor saws) as some bevel gauges can contact the blade if in the upper groove with the table steeply tilted.

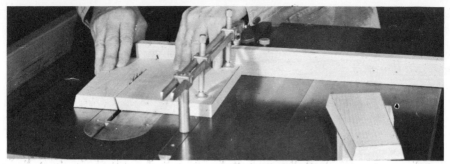

Bevel cut is being made here on a saw with a tilting blade. Work is guided through saw by the miter gauge, which is faced with wood and equipped with clamp-down attachment. *Courtesy Rockwell Mfg. Co.*

Miter Cutting is as simple as square crosscutting, but the miter gauge is set at an angle (45 degrees in standard work) and locked. Although the gauge may be swung in either direction to guide the angle cut, it is generally better to set it so its trailing end points toward the saw blade rather than away from it. This makes it easier to hold the work firm during the cut. If the metal miter gauge is used "as is" the work tends to creep toward the blade in this type of cut. This results in a slightly off-angle cut. To prevent it, attach a wood facing to the gauge with flathead bolts. (Most miter gauges have holes provided for this purpose.) Wood screws may be turned through the wood face from the back so their points just protrude on the side that contacts the work. These screw points, called "anchor points," stick into the work just enough to provide a nonskid grip and prevent creeping. The wood facing should be longer than the miter gauge itself, thus providing more contact surface for large pieces.

Grooving can be done with the saw blade alone, or more easily with a dado head. The latter typically consists of two outside saw blades and three or four inside cutters that can be placed between them. Various combinations of saws and cutters provide a range of groove-cutting widths from ⅛" to about $1\frac{3}{16}$" with an average unit. The depth of the groove is regulated by adjusting the distance the cutting teeth protrude above the table. Once the dado head is assembled for the desired width and set for the required depth,

Cutting a groove on the table saw with a dado head of two outside blades with cutters set between them. Cut is completed in a single pass. *Courtesy Rockwell Mfg. Co.*

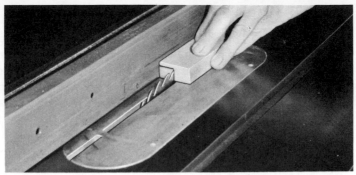

Cutting a rabbet with the saw blade alone requires two passes. The dimensions of the rabbet are controlled by the fence. *Courtesy Rockwell Mfg. Co.*

it completes the groove in a single pass, assuming a normal groove depth. The same unit is used to cut tenons. If the full width of the blade and cutter combination is less than the tenon length, make the first cut at the inner end of the tenon, then work toward the end.

To cut a groove with the saw blade alone, set the fence first so the blade cuts one side of the groove. Then set it to cut the other side. A series of closely spaced intermediate cuts are then made in successive passes. If a few wafer-thin sections of wood remain between the cuts they are easily broken out. The bottom of the groove may then be smoothed by a few shave cuts with a chisel. Where the groove is narrow the intermediate cuts may be overlapped so all wood is removed, completing the work with saw alone.

Rabbeting is simply cutting a groove into a corner of a piece of wood rather than into its surface. If a dado head is used it can be done in a single pass, as in grooving. If it is done with the saw blade alone, it requires two passes. The dimensions of the rabbet are controlled by the fence. Set it first to cut inward from the edge of a board, and run the board through the saw on edge. Then set the fence to make the cut inward from the board surface to meet the first cut at the inner corner of the rabbet. For the smoothest corner, make the first cut just a little shy of full depth, and allow the second cut to clean out the corner. As the cut-out piece is left completely free between the blade and the fence, it may be shot back toward the operator by blade friction, so be sure to stand to one side in this type of work. If the surface cut is made first and the edge cut second, the cut-out piece will be on the outside of the blade, not likely to be shot backward. But if the piece is short and the slot in the saw table wide, there's danger of the work dropping into the slot. Your best bet: suit the method to the job.

Coving is the process of cutting a rounded groove with the table saw. To visualize the process, suppose you remove the saw's regular fence and clamp a wooden one across the saw table, not parallel to the blade, as usual, but at right angles to it. Now set the saw blade to project only about ⅛″ above the table and push the work *across* the blade. The result will be a rounded gutter ⅛″ deep in the wood surface. Raise the blade another ⅛″ for a second pass and your gutter is ¼″ deep and wider. The curve of the gutter is, of course, the same as the perimeter of the saw blade.

In practice, the work is rarely run across the blade at right angles, but rather at a long angle to it. This provides greater cove depth with less width, and allows the saw blade to function in more normal manner. To plan the depth and width of the cove, set the saw blade to extend above the table the full cove depth. Then use a set of parallel rules so that one rule is just touching the front edge of the blade, the other the back edge. Swing the rules around until the space between them (while still contacting the blade edges) is the cove width you want. Then clamp your wooden coving fence at the same angle.

In all coving work start with not more than ⅛″ blade projection, and increase it only by ⅛″ increments. Favor a small blade over a large one, and plan on sanding for a final finish. To ease the work you can start by making a series of close parallel cuts along the regular fence (parallel to the blade) to remove the bulk of the material from the cove path. This calls for the deepest cut in the center, progresively shallower cuts (within the planned cove outline) toward the edges. This step is helpful in making large coves or coves in hardwood.

Taper Cutting. To understand how this is done, begin with ordinary ripping. The work is held against the fence and pushed through the saw. The work emerges from the saw parallel-sided. Now place another piece between the work and the saw fence. Suppose this other piece has a small block nailed to one end, so as to hold the work at an angle to the saw blade rather than parallel to it. Now push the work through the saw, holding it against the blocked-out piece as that piece slides along the fence. The work is now at an angle to the saw blade so the blade will cut it at an angle—the first cut of a taper. After the long wedge-shaped piece is cut from this first side it may be turned over to cut a similar piece from the opposite side. But, since a wedge-shaped piece has already been removed from the first side, it must be blocked out twice as far to cut the same shaped piece from the opposite side. To do this the easiest way you make a "step block" and nail it to the end of the guide board that slides against the fence. The first step blocks the work out a distance equal to the amount of taper you want on one side of the work. The second step blocks it out twice that distance for tapering the opposite side. If you want to taper a 2″-square table leg down to 1″ square at the base, for example, you make the first step in your step block ½″, the second one 1″. This tapers ½″ from each side, working first on the ½″ step, then the 1″ step for the opposite side.

Crosscutting to Exact Length. When only one piece of stock is to be cut to length, it can be done simply by marking the edge that enters the saw and the adjoining top surface. Then the work is guided through the saw by the miter gauge. When a number of parts must be cut in succession to exactly the same length there are several methods of doing it. The stop rod that fits into most miter gauges is one of the simplest devices for the purpose. This consists of a straight rod that is held in a hole in the end of the miter gauge by a setscrew, and an L-shaped rod held to the straight one by a wingnut clamp. To use it you slide the L-shaped rod out until the distance from the L bend to

Stop rod attached to the miter gauge being used to cut a number of pieces to the same length. L-shaped rod, clamped at desired distance from saw blade, regulates length of cut.

Stop block clamped to rip fence the correct distance from saw blade regulates length of cut, prevents cut-off piece from jamming against fence as work moves through the saw.

Stop block can also be clamped to wood facing of miter gauge at proper distance from blade to regulate length of cut. Work is butted against block and moved into blade by the miter gauge.

Here stop block clamped to table at proper distance from blade regulates cut. Work is butted against block, guided through saw by miter gauge equipped with clamp-down attachment.

the saw blade is the length you want cut, then clamp it tight. Set the wood to be cut so one end seats against the L bend. Push the miter gauge forward to run the work through the saw, and it will be cut to the set length, as will each successive piece. *Always* use the stop rod so as to hold the supported part of the work, that is, the part being pushed by the miter gauge. Never use it on the free, or cut off end. If you do, it tends to swing the free piece at an angle after cutting, jamming it against the saw so that it may be kicked back at you.

Another method of cutting numerous pieces to the same length involves the use of the fence. Pull the miter gauge back clear of the saw and clamp a wood block to the fence directly opposite the miter gauge. Then set the fence so that a piece of wood held against the miter gauge and butted against the block clamped to the fence will be cut to the desired length when run through the saw. Note that when the work is pushed forward toward the saw, the end that was seated against the block passes off of the block and moves along with block-thickness clearance between it and the fence. This prevents jamming against the fence after cut-off. Never use the fence alone (without the block) for fixed-length crosscutting. Jamming of the cut off pieces between blade and fence is almost certain without the clearance provided by the starting block.

Several other methods are also possible. If you have a wood facing on your miter gauge, for example, you can attach a stop block to it to set the length of pieces being cut. Or you can clamp a block to the saw table at the starting point of the miter gauge travel. A piece held against the miter gauge and butted against the block will then be cut to the set length. It passes off the block as it moves toward the saw, so there is no jamming.

General Sawing Information. Crosscutting accuracy benefits from the use of a wood facing on the miter gauge, not only from the anchor pins that can be used to prevent creeping, but from the cut the saw makes through the wood facing. If you line up the cutting line on the work with the saw cut in the wood facing your cut will be exact.

The wood facing also permits the use of guide pins for spacing slots or notch cuts an equal distance apart. Suppose you want to space a series of shallow cuts ½″ apart along the edge or surface of a board. (This type of cut is often used in making spacers for record cabinets.) You simply drive a nail or screw of a diameter equal to the saw cut width (kerf) into the facing at a distance of ½″ from the blade. Allow for the set of the saw teeth. Easiest way: simply measure out from the saw cut in the facing. To start grooving or notching, set the end of the work against the guide pin and run the work through the saw. The first cut will be ½″ from the end. Now move the work out so that this first cut drops over the guide pin, and run the work through the saw again. The second cut will be exactly ½″ from the first. Repeat the process all the way along to make your series of evenly spaced cuts.

The same method is used in making box joints. These are the joints in which a series of short tenons from one piece fit into matching notches of the other. To make this type of joint a dado head is used in place of the saw blade. A small wooden guide block equal in width to the notches is fastened to the miter gauge facing in place of a guide pin. Then the two joint parts are held together offset by the width of one notch, and run through the saw repeatedly, advancing a notch at a time, as in the guide pin cutting described previously. It is essential, of course, that the work be planned so tenons and notches are equal in width. This is simply a matter of spacing the guide block one block width out from the blade.

In all regular crosscutting and ripping you can reduce blade friction by adjusting your blade to protrude only about ¼″ above the surface of the work being cut. This is ample for through cutting, and it reduces the blade area in contact with the wood. As to sawdust, most saws have an opening in the lower blade housing through which the saw dust is emitted. Cut a small cardboard carton to fit over this hole so the sawdust will be directed into it. Cut a somewhat larger hole in the top of the carton and cover it with a layer or two of cheesecloth. The fast-turning saw blade acts like a blower to some extent, providing a slight air stream along with the momentum of the sawdust. The cheesecloth provides an air escape, but sifts out the sawdust. In average work the carton need be emptied only after a day or two of use.

Saw Blades. The handiest blades for the table saw are the combination blade and the hollow-ground planer blade. Both can crosscut, rip, and miter. The combination blade is used for all average work, the planer blade for fine work where a smooth sawed surface is required. For maximum cutting

Box joint can be cut in two pieces of wood simultaneously with the aid of a guide block fastened to wood facing of miter gauge (See drawing below). Block, which is same width as notches, is spaced one notch-width from dado cutter. After each notch is cut, it is seated over guide block and next cut is made.

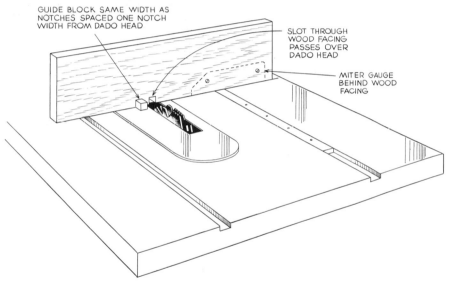

GUIDE BLOCK SAME WIDTH AS NOTCHES SPACED ONE NOTCH WIDTH FROM DADO HEAD

SLOT THROUGH WOOD FACING PASSES OVER DADO HEAD

MITER GAUGE BEHIND WOOD FACING

speed, when a lot of material is to be ripped or crosscut, you can use a rip or crosscut blade respectively. But the difference in efficiency is too small to make blade shifting worthwhile in everyday work.

Blade size. One of the most popular table saw sizes is the 8″, as the blade can handle the heaviest lumber most home shops are apt to use. But smaller sizes cover a lumber thickness range ample for shop work not involving structural thicknesses. And a small blade in a large saw sometimes does special jobs a full-sized blade can't do. In cutting very thin strips for fine model work, as in model plane and ship construction, for example, a small, fine-toothed blade is often a must. Equally important, however, is a table insert to match it. In thin-strip cutting it is important that the gap between the blade and the edges of the slot through which it protrudes be kept to a minimum. This assures support of the slender work as it passes through the saw. You can use the original table insert as a pattern for one to fit a smaller blade. Thin

Combination blade, for all-round work, does ripping, crosscutting, and mitering.

Planer does three kinds of cutting, too, but leaves smooth edge that requires no sanding.

Flooring blade, of special steel to withstand contact with nails, is for cutting up used lumber.

Plywood blade produces smooth, splinter-free cuts in any direction relative to surface veneer.

Cut-off blade is used in crosscut squaring and trimming to size. It holds keen edge over long period.

Ripping blade resembles combination blade except that backs of teeth are not beveled.

plywood is a good material for the substitute. If it can't be obtained thin enough to seat flush with the table, you can use ¼" plywood and make a panel to cover the entire saw table. Cut a slot for the saw blade with the blade itself. Simply push the new tabletop into the saw to the position it will occupy, plus about ¼" for front clearance. Then shift the panel a fraction of an inch to one side and make a second pass to provide a little extra width for blade side clearance. Clamps can hold the top in place for a small job. Or it can be bolted to the table with flathead bolts set flush in the plywood.

There are various other table saw accessories you can make if they are not available readymade. This includes table extensions for saws for which they are not available. The important rule: make it safe and solid.

Sharpening. One good guide to the basic tooth shape of a saw blade is the new blade. As an aid to future reconditioning, make a paper tracing of each new blade and keep it where you can find it. On each pattern jot down the amount of set the teeth have when new. If you haven't the tool to measure it get the data from the manufacturer. The tooth shapes of the common blades are shown in the photos. Sharpening procedure is generally similar to that for hand saws. You'll need a clamp for the blade. This can be made from wood with two halves hinged so a bolt can be passed through both halves and the center hole of the saw to hold it. The entire unit can then be gripped in a vise. As one portion of the blade is completed, loosen the bolt and rotate the saw to bring the next portion into working position.

You'll need a 6″ or 7″ taper file for crosscut saws (of typical workshop size), a 7″ mill file with one round edge for rip and combination saws, and a round taper file for cleaning out gullets. In addition, a hand setting tool should be on tap to set the saw teeth.

The overall sharpening job is not one to be done carelessly, but it is not too critical in all details. More important than getting every angle exact is getting all teeth alike. But aim to be as precise as you can. If you're not sure you can do the job take the blade to a professional saw sharpening service. Do this also if you have trouble with a new blade. It may have been made with very slight set for smooth work in seasoned wood. And you may find it binding or smoking in the type of wood you're using. Explain your trouble to the saw sharpener, and you'll be surprised how easily he can cure it.

CHAPTER NINETEEN

THE RADIAL-ARM SAW

THE RADIAL-ARM SAW does the work of a conventional table saw but its blade cuts downward from above the table instead of upward from under the table. In its simplest form it consists of a table with a cylindrical steel column rising from the back and a sturdy arm extending outward over the table from the column. The saw and motor unit is suspended beneath the arm and rides backward or forward along tracks on the arm. The arm may be locked at right angles to the table front for square crosscutting, or swung to any angle and locked for miters and other angle cuts. The blade and motor may also be tipped to any angle for bevel cuts. The rip fence on the table does not slide, as on a table saw, but is usually fixed near the rear of the table. For ripping,

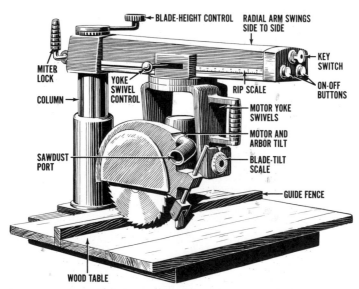

Basic parts of the radial-arm saw. Saw and motor unit rides along track in arm, which may be swung from side to side.

With chuck in place of saw blade, motor unit can be used for horizontal drilling.

With motor spindle in vertical position, sanding drum can replace blade for sanding curved edges.

With spindle horizontal, blade may be replaced with grinding wheel and guard for tool sharpening.

Motor unit set with spindle vertical uses molding cutter. Cutter works over top of fence, which guides work.

the saw and motor unit is swiveled so the blade is parallel to the fence. Then the saw is moved toward or away from the fence (along the arm's tracks) and locked in the proper place to cut the width desired.

Types of Radial-Arm Saws. The two commonest workshop varieties are the single-arm type such as the Saw Smith in the photos, and the double-arm type such as the Delta. In the single-arm machine, the arm swings to any cutting angle around the upright column. In the double-arm type the upper arm remains fixed laterally across the table, while the lower arm (pivoted from the upper-arm end) can be swung to any angle. The pros and cons of the two types are to a considerable extent a matter of individual preference. Your best bet in making a selection is to examine both and, if possible, try them.

Sizes are based on blade size, as with other types of circular saws, and generally range from 9″ (workshop size) through 10″, 12″, 14″, 16″, 18″, and 20″. The larger sizes are used mainly by lumberyards and mills. The power of a 9-incher is likely to be around ¾ to 1 h.p. A 10″ model, the largest size commonly used in the home shop, is usually in the 1 or 2 h.p. range. Practically all turn at the same speed, 3450 r.p.m. Judge the size you need by the heaviest lumber you're apt to cut.

Crosscutting. The saw and motor unit is pushed back all the way toward the column at the back of the table, then lowered so the blade will cut through the work on the table. The work is placed against the fence and held there with one hand while the saw and motor unit is pulled outward toward the front of the table. The blade cuts through the wooden fence and through the work. Also, in order to cut all the way through the work, the tips of the teeth

In crosscutting, work is held against fence and saw-motor unit pulled outward from behind fence to make cut. Blade cuts through fence, also makes shallow groove in table.

In miter and angle cutting, arm is swung to desired angle and locked. Then saw unit is pulled forward from behind fence, as in square crosscutting. Miter cuts all follow same path through fence and across table.

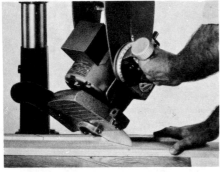

Compound angles are simple with radial-arm saw. Swing arm to crosscutting angle, then tilt motor unit to bevel angle. Lock in position and draw saw through work held against fence.

Ripping with saw inboard of motor calls for feeding work from right-hand side of table so work moves against direction of blade rotation.

leave a groove in the table. To preserve the surface of the table many radial-saw users cover it with hardboard attached with countersunk flathead screws recessed enough to avoid contact with the saw. This surfacing can be replaced at nominal cost whenever necessary. The saw does not cut through it. If this aspect of the operation creates the impression that the saw will eventually cut itself to pieces, be assured that it will not.

In making right-angle cuts the blade will always travel in the same groove through the fence and across the table. The same applies to the groove made by a miter cut. If the saw is tilted for a bevel crosscut it V-notches the wooden fence at the point where it meets the vertical cut. But the fence's usefulness is not impaired. In ripping, a series of short, shallow, parallel cuts eventually appear in the table surface from the various width ripping jobs. But the effect of these and the grooves is no more important than that of the miter-gauge grooves in the table of a conventional table saw.

The radial-arm saw has a major crosscutting advantage. You move the saw across the work instead of moving the work across the saw. If you must make a square, angled, or beveled cut across the end of a board, say, 16' long, you simply set the board against the fence with its overhanging end supported, and run the saw across it to make the cut. On a table saw you would

When saw blade is outboard of motor, as in ripping wide panel section, work must be fed from left side of table as blade rotates in opposite direction.

No makeshift fence is required for coving with radial-arm saw, as saw itself can be swung to any angle required. Work is then pushed through saw along regular fence.

have to move the 16′ board, overhanging end and all, across the saw—an awkward if not impossible job without jamming or binding. Another advantage of the radial-arm saw is the fact that the over-table blade can be easily lined up visually with a cutting line on the surface of the work. Also, as described later, it can do some things no other saw can do.

Ripping is usually done with the arm across the table at right angles to the table front. The saw and motor unit is then swiveled around parallel to the table front (ripping position) and locked. It can still ride backward or forward on the arm tracks for setting at the width of cut to be made. Then it is locked to the arm. Locking may be by knob or lever, depending on the make of saw. The work is then pushed through the saw as in regular table-saw operation.

Most radial-arm saws can be swiveled to ripping position with the blade either "inboard" (to the rear of the motor) or "outboard" (blade toward the table front, motor to the rear). On most saws this requires that the work be fed to the saw from the right side of the table in inboard ripping, from the left side in outboard ripping, in order to suit the feed to the direction of blade rotation. Feeding from the correct side is of the utmost importance as wrong-way feed is extremely dangerous. To avoid any possible error it pays to know the reasons why feed and direction of blade rotation must be properly related.

Direction of Blade Rotation. When the saw is pulled outward from the rear of the table in crosscutting, its teeth are traveling downward and rearward as they enter the work. This tends to hold the work down on the table and back against the fence. And the fence prevents the work from being driven backward off the table by the blade. When the saw and motor unit is swiveled to ripping position it is of the utmost importance that the work be fed into the blade so the teeth are traveling *toward* the work as they contact it. Most radial-arm saws have the direction of blade rotation and feed plainly marked on the blade housing. *Never* try feeding the work from the wrong side. Traveling in the same direction as the saw teeth with nothing to block it, the work is likely to be whipped forward violently and shot out from the other side of the table, with a high risk of drawing your hands into the blade.

With dado head, radial-arm saw plows or grooves at any angle. Work is held against fence, motor unit pulled from behind fence across work.

Dado head can also be used for rabbeting. As head is never used in through-cutting it cuts slot in fence but not in table surface.

Coving with the radial-arm saw is simpler than on a table saw as no make-shift fence need be clamped to the table. The work is held against the regular fence and the saw and motor unit set at the desired coving angle by swinging the motor unit and locking it in position. The work is then pushed along the fence and through the saw as in ripping. The saw may also be tilted to increase the range of cove contours. The blade should be started at a ⅛″ depth of cut and advanced by ⅛″ increments as in coving with a table saw.

Rabbeting may be done with the blade alone or with a dado head. If the blade is used the work is laid flat on the table with one edge against the fence, and the saw set to make the first cut in the work surface near the other edge. The saw is in ripping position but adjusted for the rabbet's depth of cut. To make the second cut in from the edge to meet the first one and free the rabbeted section, the saw and motor unit is tilted through 90 degrees to put the plane of the blade in horizontal position. The unit is then re-positioned along the arm to the correct depth of cut for the rabbet. The work is then pushed through the saw as usual, and the job is done. If the dado head is used, the saw and motor unit is set in the inboard ripping position, then tilted 90 degrees to put the dado head in a horizontal plane. It is moved back on the arm so that it will do its cutting over the top of the rip fence. If the work is not as high as the fence it may be blocked up on another piece of wood to bring the area of the rabbet above the fence. The dado head is then adjusted for the cut. The work is done with a single pass.

Grooving, or plowing, as it is frequently termed, is simply a matter of setting the unit so the dado head is at the desired position and depth, with the plane of the head parallel to the fence. The job may then be done with a single pass of the work through the dado head. The dado head may also be used to cut dadoes directly across the work by positioning the head as in crosscutting, or it may be swung around to cut a dado at any required angle. In this type of operation the work is held stationary on the table against the fence and the saw pushed across it.

Molding cutters are used in much the same manner as the dado head. For some types of molding, however, it may be necessary to make a temporary auxiliary table and fence to rest on top of the regular table. This permits both

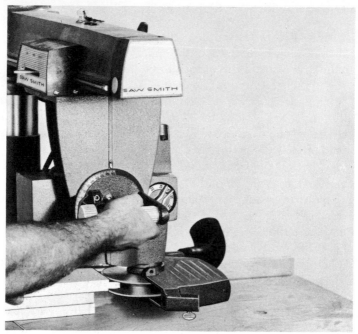

Dado head with spacers can be used with motor spindle vertical, to cut tenons in a single pass.

fence and table (auxiliary) to be cut out as required so the cutter can operate with a portion below the table surface to complete a particular molding form. The auxiliary unit can be kept for future use in the same type of work.

Routing is also possible with the radial saw. Adapters are available for most makes to take ½″ router-bit shanks. For occasional work a geared chuck is sometimes used. The motor unit is set with the spindle vertical and the business end of it down. Either straight or curved pattern routing may be done, but the bit should be set to take a cut of only about ⅛″ depth at each pass.

Straight routing is done with the aid of the fence; if a design of irregular shape is to be routed it is done with a ¼″ plywood pattern. The inner area of the pattern is cut out with a sabre saw or jigsaw so that its inner rim forms the shape to be routed. This pattern is then secured with brads to the underside of the work. An auxiliary table is used atop the regular table. A metal pin or dowel the same diameter as the router bit is set in the upper table directly under and aligned with the router bit. To rout the work, you simply lower the bit to cut to ⅛″ depth, and guide the pattern on the underside against the pin. As the router bit is directly above the pin it cuts the exact pattern outline as the pattern moves past the pin. Once the complete outline is routed the center area can be routed away with a series of freehand passes across it. There's no danger of routing through the outer rim, as the pin stops the movement of the work whenever the rim is reached in any pass.

Sanding with a disk is possible by a wide range of methods on the radial saw. The disk may be set in a vertical plane with its lower rim just above the table. An auxiliary table is then used in front of the disk to bring the work up to the disk level. For bevel sanding, the motor unit may be tilted to any angle required. For surface sanding, the spindle is set vertically, and the unit lowered so the disk rests on the surface to be sanded. The work may then be pushed along the fence to guide it past the disk.

Drum sanding, not possible on a table saw, is easy on the radial saw. The common drum sizes are 3″ long by 3″ in diameter, and 2″ long by 1¾″ in diameter. The core of the drum is rubber with a metal shaft through its center. The lower end of the shaft is threaded and fitted with a large washer and nut. When the nut is tightened the added pressure expands the rubber to grip the abrasive sleeve that fits around it. The upper end of the shaft is coupled to the saw spindle by an adapter or chuck. This is the type of sander to use in sanding curved edges. Be sure to keep the work moving over the drum as any hesitation results in the drum cutting a hollow in the work. The saw spindle may be set in the most convenient position for the type of work being sanded. Most work, however, can be done with the spindle vertical and the drum set just above the table surface. So that the lower edge of the work will be sanded a small scrap wood pad may be nailed to the table to raise the work slightly.

Drilling and Boring are operations that are not possible with a table saw but are also easy with the radial saw. The motor unit is set with its spindle horizontal and parallel to the fence. Its height above the table and distance from the fence are set to position the hole in the work at the desired location. If necessary, the work may be blocked up from the table, as the motor housing prevents the spindle from being lowered beyond a certain point. A geared chuck on the spindle takes the drill bit. The work is then simply pushed along the fence and into the drill. In some types of drilling the work may be set against the fence and the motor unit pushed along the track to run the bit into the work. Angle drilling, of course, is simply a matter of setting the spindle to the angle required.

Limitations of the Radial-Arm Saw. Although this tool can do the work of the table saw plus that of numerous other power tools, it is limited in the size panel it can cut. The maximum distance possible between saw blade and the rearmost position of the fence sets the limit. The upright column determines the rearmost fence location. The table saw, on the other hand, has no column rising from the table. Hence, with table extensions, it can cut through the center of the largest panels commonly handled in the home shop. In selecting one type of saw or the other weigh these factors as they apply to the type of work you plan to do.

CHAPTER TWENTY

THE DRILL PRESS

THE DRILL PRESS is the one tool in the shop that can actually bore square holes. It can also bore round holes, do sanding, planing, routing, carving, gem cutting and polishing, and it can shine your shoes. In short, it is a far more versatile tool than many of its users realize. In everyday use, however, it is used most for its primary purpose: boring holes perpendicular to the surface of the work or at a pre-set angle to it.

In its usual form the drill press consists of a heavy metal base with a

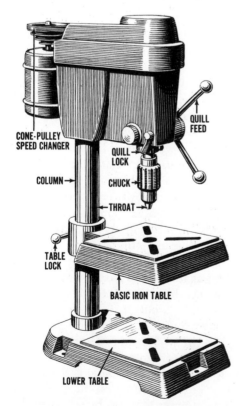

Basic parts of the drill press. Lower table, called the base, is used to support the work when it's necessary to get maximum space below the chuck. The basic table is then swung around out of the way.

cylindrical steel column rising from the back to support the drill-press "head." The head contains the motor, the step pulleys that regulate speed, and the spindle that carries the drill chuck as its lower end. Between the base and head is the table on which the work is placed. This can be raised or lowered on the column and locked by a clamping lever at any desired height. On many models the head can be raised and lowered in similar fashion. The simpler "drill-press stand" that converts a portable power drill to a drill press uses the base as the table. The head that contains the clamped-in power drill is raised or lowered to bring the drill bit to proper starting position above the work. Newest of drill-press forms is the radial-arm type that permits the head to be moved in or out from the column, to be swung to any angle for drilling and for a wide variety of other operations.

The spindle, on a conventional drill press, is the vertical shaft that carries the chuck and turns the drill bit. It is housed in a cylindrical sleeve called the "quill" which has a bearing at top and bottom in which the spindle revolves. A toothed rack on the quill and a pinion in the head move quill and spindle up or down. The step pulley that drives the spindle does not move up and down with the spindle, however, as this would shift the drive belts out of alignment. It remains at fixed level while a keyed or splined section of the spindle slides up or down through the pulley hub.

How to Use the Drill Press. Start by mounting the drill bit in the chuck and setting the belt on the step pulleys to get the required drilling speed. The chart shows typical drilling speeds for common materials and drill sizes. Then place the work on the table and bring the drill bit tip just above it by raising or lowering the table, the drill press head, or both, depending on the job and the most convenient working position.

The location of the center of the hole to be drilled should be plainly marked and preferably awl-indented in wood, definitely center-punched in metal. If the work is wood and of convenient size and shape for gripping it may be hand held. But small pieces and most metal work should be clamped. The reason: the bit may "grab" and spin the work with possible injury to the hands. Regular C-clamps or hand screws may be used for clamping. Or bolts may be run down through the slots in the drill press table to hold the work in place by means of scrap-wood battens tightened down on it. Most drill-press tables have these slots, though their size and arrangement varies.

A downward pull on the quill feed sends the drill bit through the work. The feed may be a single lever or several levers radiating from a hub like spokes. A spring lifts it when released. Most drill-press tables have a center hole in them to allow passage of the drill bit as it emerges from the underside of the work. If the table does not have such a hole or if the table must be shifted (to accommodate the work) so the hole is out of line with the drill bit, a piece of scrap wood must be used under the work to take the emerging bit. This is always a good practice anyway in woodworking as it prevents the emerging bit from splitting out the surface on the underside of the work.

Cutting to fixed depth is a simple matter when a single hole is the job at hand, as most drill presses have graduations in inches either on the quill itself or on the hub of the quill feed. Many have a pointer that can be set when the

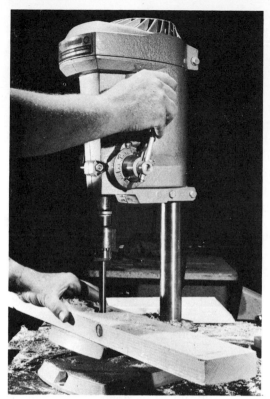
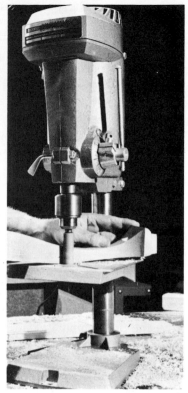

Quill-feed lever is pulled forward and down to lower bit into work. Graduations around hub of feed are marked in inches to show depth of drill penetration; pointer shows when depth has been reached.

For drum sanding on drill press, drum is set close to table surface. Small drum may revolve partly in table's center hole. Work is moved against direction of rotation.

drill bit is just seated against the work. The advance of the drill can then be gauged exactly as the graduations move past the pointer.

When a series of holes are to be drilled to the same depth the best method consists of using a stop rod with adjustable stop nuts. One end of the rod is clamped to the lower portion of the quill. The other end runs upward through a bracket on the drill-press head. As the quill descends, advancing the drill into the work, the upper end of the stop rod moves downward with it, stopping the quill when the stop nut on the rod contacts the bracket on the drill-press head. This is one system used on many presses. Similar mechanisms are used on others, though some have no stop arrangement. It is often possible to rig your own on these, however. For sanding and routing and other operations requiring the quill to remain in fixed position a clamping device is provided on most models. On all, a return spring lifts the quill after drilling.

Where a series of holes must be drilled in a straight line a wood fence may be clamped to the drill-press table so that work may be slid along it. This assures all holes will be the same distance from the edge of the work, hence in a straight line.

Drilling pressure varies with the job and is largely a matter of "feel." It should be sufficient to keep the drill cutting (you can tell by the chips coming out of the hole) but it should not be so much as to "force" the bit. You can quickly sense the pressure at which the bit is working efficiently—usually light to moderate pressure.

The tilting table is not found on all drill presses but is handy when present as it permits the table to be set at any desired angle so work clamped to it can be drilled accordingly. Where angle drilling is required on a drill press not having this feature, the work can be blocked up and clamped with scrap wood to achieve the same results. A drill-press vise, easily held by hand on the drill-press table for most work, provides a firm grip on round work in either horizontal or vertical position. For heavy work or repeat-drilling jobs it can be bolted in place through the slots in the table.

Drum Sanding is done simply by replacing the drill bit with a sanding drum with its shank held in the chuck. The drum is brought down close to the table surface and the work slid over it along the top of the table. This is a handy accessory for sanding curved edges.

Surface Sanding utilizes small disk sanders of the Swirlaway type. They are brought into contact with the surface to be sanded and the drill press is locked at that position. Then the work is moved steadily under the sander with the press running. Planing attachments are available for use in similar fashion.

Routing is done with router bits mounted in place of drill bits and turning at not less than about 3400 r.p.m. If the drill press has a speed of 5000 r.p.m. it is better for routing. The routing should always be done against a guide or a fence which can be made easily of wood and clamped in place. Always feed the work from the left-hand side of the table toward the right so the rotation of the router bit will tend to hold the work against the fence. Then the part that is actually cutting the wood is traveling toward the fence. On the other half of its revolution it is traveling back across the open cut already made. The left-to-right feed is based on the assumption that the fence is behind the bit, as is usually the case. The routing should be done so as to make a ⅛″ deep cut on the first pass and to increase the depth by that amount with each successive pass until the desired depth is reached. This is done by advancing the bit to the depth for the pass, then stopping the drill press and locking the quill at that depth. Then the press is restarted and the work moved along to make the full length of the cut. Router bits are often available from the hardware dealer from whom the drill press is obtained; if not, through the manufacturer.

Grinding on the drill press is merely a matter of mounting the shank of a grinding-wheel arbor in place of the drill bit and setting the speed well within the maximum r.p.m. printed on the grinding wheel. A metal or wood guard can be shaped to shield the wheel as in conventional grinding rigs. Sharpening methods are generally the same, adapted to the horizontal plane of the wheel. While the grinding capabilities of the drill press are not as broad as those of a conventional grinder (or one driven by a portable power drill) they can often save the day when no other grinding equipment is available.

Gem Cutting and Polishing are other operations possible on the drill press.

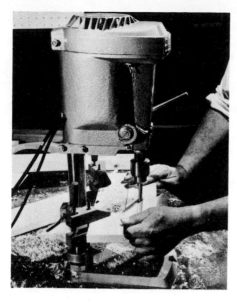

When routing on drill press, wood fence is clamped to table with hand screws to serve as guide for straight-line routing. Work is fed from left to right, taking ⅛" depth of cut with each pass.

The actual cutting requires a 50-grit 6" diamond saw which can be mounted on an arbor chucked in the drill press. If you start with "preforms," which are stones already rough ground to form, you can skip the diamond saw. The succeeding steps in grinding and polishing are done against the upper flat sides of abrasive wheels mounted on arbors turned by the drill-press spindle. A large basin should be set on the drill-press table under the grinding wheel so a trickle of water can be flowed on the wheel surface, as the work is done wet. Start with a 100-grit wheel running at 1200 to 2400 r.p.m. and finish shaping with a 220-grit wheel at the same speed.

Polishing is done with 220-grit abrasive cloth tacked to a wood wheel with a felt base under the abrasive cloth. This adapts to the contour of the stone (if rounded). This stage is done dry at about 1200 r.p.m. Final polishing is done with F-grit silicon-carbide powder, or Tripoli. The underside of the stone is bonded to a pencil-length piece of dowel with lapidary cement so it can be handled easily during the steps of the process. If you plan this type of work you will want to go into various other details of it. The basic procedure described, however, will get you started and enable you to plan the necessary drill-press adaptations.

Boring Square Holes. It is a simple matter to bore square holes, as in mortising, with the drill press. An attachment called a hollow chisel is the device that makes it possible. Essentially, this is a square steel tube with the edges of its lower end sharpened. A bit similar to an auger bit turns inside it and projects about $\frac{1}{16}$" below the bottom of the hollow chisel. The hollow chisel, itself, is clamped to the quill of the drill press with an accessory made for the purpose. The bit that turns inside it is attached to the spindle by a sleeve with setscrews, as the usual chuck would be too large to fit in the clamping accessory.

In use, the mortising chisel, as it is commonly termed, is first lined up with the outline of the mortise on the work. Then the drill press is started and the hollow-chisel-bit unit brought down into the work with the quill feed as in regular drilling. As the bit bores into the wood the hollow chisel follows, squaring the hole. As the bit removes most of the material only slight additional pressure on the quill feed is needed to force the hollow chisel into the hole. The chips produced by the revolving bit are carried up the inside of the chisel by the spiral of the bit flutes, and emitted through a hole in the side of the hollow chisel.

Where a mortise larger than the hollow chisel must be made the square-hole boring procedure is simply repeated in a line or in several lines overlapping each other to make the overall hole size required.

Drilling Metal. A lubricant is usually required when drilling metal to prevent overheating the bit. While a simple shot of light oil is usually all that is necessary for a quick job on thin material, deep drilling calls for the lubricant best suited to the material. The following list will assure the best results:

Material	Lubricant
Hard, tough steels	Turpentine or kerosene
Softer steels	Lard oil or similar oil
Aluminum, other soft alloys	Kerosene
Brass	Dry or paraffin oil
Die castings	Dry or kerosene
Cast iron	Dry (no lubricant)

Whatever material is being drilled, the drill-bit diameter, the material and speed should be matched as closely as possible, according to the following chart:

Drill Diam.	Soft Metals	Plastics Hard Rubber	Annealed Cast Iron	Mild Steel	Malleable Iron	Hard Cast Iron	Tool or Hard Steel	Steel Alloy
1/16	18320	12217	8554	6111	5500	4889	3667	2445
3/32	12212	8142	5702	4071	3666	3528	2442	1649
1/8	9160	6112	4278	3056	2750	2445	1833	1222
5/32	7328	4888	3420	2444	2198	1954	1465	977
3/16	6106	4075	2852	2037	1833	1630	1222	815
7/32	5234	3490	2444	1745	1575	1396	1047	698
1/4	4575	3055	2139	1527	1375	1222	917	611
9/32	4071	2712	1900	1356	1222	1084	814	542
5/16	3660	2445	1711	1222	1100	978	733	489
11/32	3330	2220	1554	1110	1000	888	666	444
3/8	3050	2037	1426	1018	917	815	611	407
13/32	2818	1878	1316	939	846	752	563	376
7/16	2614	1746	1222	873	786	698	524	349
15/32	2442	1628	1140	814	732	652	488	326
1/2	2287	1528	1070	764	688	611	458	306
9/16	2035	1357	950	678	611	543	407	271
5/8	1830	1222	856	611	550	489	367	244
11/16	1665	1110	777	555	500	444	333	222
3/4	1525	1018	713	509	458	407	306	204

To change speed of drill-press spindle to suit drill size and material being drilled, pulley belt is shifted from one step on pulley to another.

The figures given are for high-speed drill bits. For carbon bits use half the speed. As all the speeds listed are not necessarily obtainable on all drill presses use the speed nearest to the one given. The speeds are based on the number of feet per minute that the perimeter of the bit is traveling. To figure the r.p.m. for any size bit, here are the recommended speeds in feet per minute of the materials listed: Soft metals, 300 f.p.m.; plastics and hard rubber, 200 f.p.m.; annealed cast iron, 140 f.p.m.; mild steel, 100 f.p.m.; malleable iron, 90 f.p.m.; hard cast iron, 80 f.p.m.; tool or hard steel, 60 f.p.m.; alloy steel or cast steel, 40 f.p.m.

Utilizing the speeds. The range of speeds possible with a typical drill press is usually limited to a relatively small portion of those listed, but adequate for commonly used materials. As can be noted from the fact that carbon drill bits are used at half the speed recommended for high-speed drills, the speeds are not criticial. There are many off-beat uses for both the high and low ranges, however. For example, a paint mixing rod is available for some drill presses to be used at low r.p.m. A buffing bonnet can be used on almost any drill press in the high-speed range for polishing any work that can be handled on the press table, including silverware and shoes. Many other drill-press applications will suggest themselves. Safety of operation should be the criterion in deciding their practicability. In all work with the drill press follow the usual rule and do not wear loose or dangling clothing, particularly a necktie.

CHAPTER TWENTY-ONE

LATHES

THE WOOD LATHE is primarily a tool for making round forms in wood. Its operating principle is simple. It spins the wood at high speed while a sharp "turning chisel" is held against it, shearing off the corners and rounding the wood as the work progresses. From there on, various shapes of chisels may be used to work an almost endless variety of contours into the wood, such as those often seen in furniture legs and bed posts.

In its earliest form the wood lathe consisted of two trees with a sharp point mounted on each one to serve as end bearings for a log supported between them. The log was rotated first one way, then the other, by a man pulling

Basic parts of a typical wood lathe. Bed gap next to headstock, not present on all wood lathes, allows turning large-diameter work on faceplate.

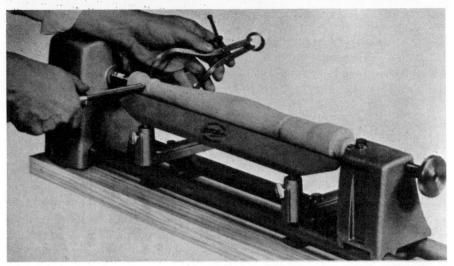

Turning long piece like this table leg is called spindle turning or turning between centers. Outside caliper is being used to measure diameter of section being cut by chisel. Beginners should always hold tool with both hands, set it aside and stop lathe before calipering.

on the ends of a cord wrapped around it. A second man held a cutting tool between his feet and guided it with his hands to smooth and round the log and work ornamental contours into it.

Today, lathes rotate in one direction only while work is being turned. The direction of rotation is such that the surface of the work being turned travels downward at the front of the lathe where the operator stands. Thus a tool rest mounted in front of the work can support a turning chisel being used to round and shape the work.

The *headstock* of the lathe, which contains the motor-driven spindle, is always on the left-hand end of the lathe as faced from the front. Several devices may be fitted to the spindle to grip the work so that it will spin with the spindle. The speed of rotation is regulated by a step pulley on the spindle and another on the motor. These pulley wheels are made up of three or four different diameter units, and mounted so that the large diameter of the lathe pulley is aligned with the small diameter of the motor pulley. Thus, by shifting the V-belt from one pulley step to another the speed of the lathe can be regulated. When the V-belt runs from the large end of the motor pulley to the small end of the lathe pulley the lathe runs faster than the motor. When the V-belt is in the opposite position the lathe runs more slowly than the motor.

The *spindle* is usually hollow and tapered internally at the right-hand end so that taper-shanked fittings will grip firmly when inserted in it. It is also threaded on the outside so that other fittings can be screwed on to it.

The *spur center* is one of the fittings commonly inserted in the spindle. This has a sharp point protruding from its center and four "spurs" spaced 90 degrees apart around it. Its purpose is to grip the end of a piece of wood to turn it. There are other types of "live" centers for use on the headstock spindle, but this is one of the handiest.

The *faceplate* is a heavy metal disk that screws on the outside thread of the spindle. It varies in form, but always has slots, holes, or both through it to permit fastening the work to it. It is used for work the spur center can't handle, such as turning large bowls.

The *lathe bed* is the long portion of the lathe extending to the right from the headstock. It is topped by smooth tracks called "ways" along which the tool rest and tailstock may be moved and locked in position.

The *tailstock*, always located to the right of the headstock, contains the "dead center" which is often in the form of a "cup center," so named because of its shape. The plain dead center is simply a conical steel point with a tapered shank to fit the hollow tailstock spindle. The cup center has a smaller point surrounded by a rim. This is the type commonly used on wood. The work is mounted between the spur center (which drives it) and the dead or cup center which acts as a bearing at the tailstock end. A drop of oil on the tailstock center keeps it from overheating from friction with the wood. A hole is made for it with an awl in soft wood or with a small drill in hardwood. In mounting the work the tailstock feed wheel is turned to move the center into the wood and eliminate end play. It is customary to move it in while turning the work by hand. When the work becomes hard to turn, back out the center by turning the feed wheel back about a quarter turn, then lock it with the spindle clamp.

The *tool rest* is clamped where required along the ways. It may be set parallel to or across the ways and moved as required to clear the work being turned. The flat metal bar on which the tools actually rest may also be adjusted up or down.

How to Make a Turning. Starting with a length of square stock, make diagonal cuts about ⅛″ deep at the headstock end of the work, and drill a small, shallow hole where they intersect at the center. Next, place the center point of the spur center in the hole and tap it with a mallet so the spurs enter the cross cuts, making visible indentations. (*Do not* do this job by hammering the wood against the spur center with the center in the lathe.) At the other end of the work locate the center with clear diagonal pencil lines and make a center hole with a punch or large awl. Now insert the spur center in the hollow spindle and fit the work on it so the spurs go into the indentations they made when tapped into the wood. At the other end, slide the tailstock up until its dead center enters the punch hole in the work, and lock it in place with its clamping knob or lever. Turn the lathe spindle by hand (you can usually do it by turning the pulley) as you advance the tailstock feed. When the headstock spindle becomes difficult to turn, back off the tailstock feed about a quarter turn and lock it. With a drop of oil on the dead center you are ready to go, after the tool rest is set.

Set the tool rest ⅛″ to ³⁄₁₆″ away from the work and about ⅛″ above the center line. Lock the adjustments and turn the work by hand to make sure all corners clear the rest. Rough the work to shape at about 1250 r.p.m. on softwood of, say, 2″ diameter, slightly slower on hardwood. But the speed difference between the two isn't critical. Larger diameters call for lower speeds, as shown in the chart. And, as indicated, the speed is increased for finishing cuts and sanding. It's easy to figure lathe speed from motor speed. Multiply the motor speed by its pulley diameter in inches and divide the product by the diameter of the pulley on the lathe. A 1750-r.p.m. motor with a 3″ pulley, for example, gives a product of 5250. With a 2″ pulley on the lathe you divide by 2 and get 2625, a good speed for general finishing. For roughing you'd use a slightly larger pulley on the lathe than on the motor to step the speed down. If the exact speed charted can't be matched with your pulley combinations use the nearest speed that can be worked out.

The Turning Chisels. For roughing out the outline of the work you use a gouge, tilted slightly in the direction it is moving along the stock. In general you work from the center toward the ends, never starting a cut at an end and working toward the center. It works nicely in stages. For example, start the cut about 2″ from the tailstock end and work toward and off the tailstock end. Then start the next bite two or three inches to the left of the point where the first one started and work toward the tailstock again until the two cuts merge. Keep this up until you are about 2″ from the headstock end, then work the other way (toward the headstock) and off that end. This way your turning chisel won't rip out large slivers as it might with one long continuous cut.

Finishing cuts are made with the skew chisel, taking a very fine shaving. You can also use an ordinary block plane set for a light cut and held at about 45 degrees to the axis of the work. A variety of other turning-chisel shapes are used (commonly about eight in a full set) for forming the ornamental turned contours. These include several narrower gouges, and a pointed "parting" chisel for cutting off or making straight inward cuts. In general, a tool is used where its blade shape is adapted to the contour being turned.

Turning an Oval is possible by mounting the work off center. First, locate the actual center of the stock at each end and punch each for mounting in the lathe. Then, on a line through the center and perpendicular to one of the surfaces of the stock, make an "off-center" mark on each side of the actual center, the two new marks equidistant from the actual center. Do this in matching position on both ends, and punch all centers for mounting. To start turning an oval form mount the work on corresponding "off centers" at each end, these being on the same side of the actual center. When the work is turned in the lathe with this off-center mounting, the turning chisel takes off stock from the side of the work that projects most, not contacting the other side. After this cut has reached the center of the two sides (of the square stock) on which it ends, the work is remounted in the other off-center holes at each end, causing the other side to project for contact with the turning chisel. When the turning process is repeated the tool shears off the second side, forming an elipse. Now, if the work is re-mounted once more on the actual centers the pointed ends of the elipse will be rounded. If this final remounting is done slightly off center (matched at each end), the next turning will round one of the pointed elipse ends and skip the other, forming a generally "streamlined" shape such as might be used for a flag or light staff of a boat. This type of turning is just one of the many special working methods possible with a lathe.

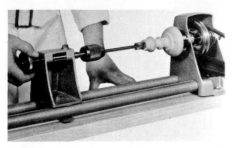 

Drilling and boring on lathe calls for drill chuck mounted on tailstock spindle. The work turns, and the drill is advanced into the work by tailstock feed wheel.

Hole is often bored before final trimming and finishing to allow ample stock around hole while boring. Here, final smoothing cut (before sanding) is taken with skew chisel.

Drilling and Boring on the lathe is a simple matter of mounting the work so it turns with the headstock spindle (either on spur center or faceplate) and mounting the drill bit in a chuck mounted in the tailstock. Thus the work turns and the drill stands still, but the result is the same as a drill bit turning into stationary work. It is essential to use some turning tool to make a small center indentation in the work to start the drill bit. This method of drilling and boring has an advantage over other methods in that the hole is automatically centered in the stock—important when the outer perimeter of the stock is not much larger than the hole, as in the case of many slender wooden candlesticks.

The Slide Rest, though not a regular part of the wood lathe's equipment, is available for many makes. This device adapts the lathe to quite a few types of metal turning, a valuable addition for craftsmen who want to work in more than one material. The slide rest is mounted on the lathe ways like the regular tool rest, but wood-turning chisels are not used. Instead, a hard steel cutting tool is clamped in the tool holder of the slide rest and fed into the work (to relatively shallow cutting depth) by a crank handle on the "cross feed" which moves the cutter into the work. Then the tool is moved along the work by the "longitudinal feed" handle. Both actuate screw feed mechanisms. The metal-turning feature is often handy when it is necessary to reduce the diameter of a rod to be used as a hinge pin, bolt, or other similar part.

Lathe Filing is a method of reducing diameter and smoothing metal without a slide rest. This is done by holding a file down on a metal rod or tube being turned in the lathe. For the best finish a "lathe file" should be used. This file has single-cut teeth at a longer angle than other files, providing for a fast but smooth cut. These are sometimes called long angle files. The effect of the long angle is to prevent clogging and chattering. The edges of the file are also commonly "safe" (without teeth) so as not to cut into any shoulders of the work that are not to be filed. Naturally, this method is not as precise as that possible with the slide rest, but adequate for many workshop jobs.

Sanding and Polishing of work in the lathe is easy. The usual successive abrasive paper grades are used, or better, abrasive cloth strip. The abrasive material should be cut into convenient lengths so that the front end of the strip can be held with one hand, the back end with the other. The center of the strip is kept in contact with the revolving work by the downward pressure of the hands on the strip ends. The strip is kept moving longitudinally along the work. Do not wrap the strip around the work and attempt to hold both ends with one hand. This can result in the abrasive strip catching and wrapping around the work with such suddenness that the hand may be slammed into the work with enough force to cause serious injury.

In general the lower lathe speeds are used for roughing and cutting, the higher ones for sanding and finishing. Wax may be applied to the work while the lathe is stopped, allowed to dry, then polished by soft cloth (sanding fashion) as the lathe runs at low speed. Hard wax in bars or blocks (like Carnauba wax) may be held against the work at low speed so friction softens the wax and causes it to adhere. It may then be cloth-polished. Metal may be brought to a mirror finish by using successive grades of abrasive cloth followed by jewellers' rouge on a cloth.

Lathe-Turning to Plan calls for a clear design on paper, a template, and a pair of outside calipers. The first step is making the cardboard template from the drawn design. This template is simply an accurate scissor-cut outline representing one half of the turned form. When the form has been accurately turned the template will fit into the contours exactly. It is a half-section of the design.

To start, turn the stock to round form matching the largest diameter of the design, finishing to this dimension with a skew chisel to leave the surface smooth enough to take pencil marks. Then hold the template against the work and make heavy pencil marks about half an inch long around the work at points where the first inward cuts are to be made. These lines need not be made all the way around as they will appear to be so anyway when the lathe is turning. Make each cut to slight depth (with the template hanging up behind the lathe in plain view) and then hold the template almost in contact with the work to check the contours and note the direction and curvature along which the cuts should proceed. Minor variations will not be noticeable, but it is wise to try this procedure on a scrap piece of stock before undertaking an actual project. The knack comes quickly.

When you are working with a template made from an existing turning, the outside caliper is handy for measuring diameters as the work progresses.

Large faceplate turnings like bowls require positioning tool rest crosswise on lathe ways. If bowl bottom is to be thick, bowl can be mounted with screws to faceplate; otherwise, scrap stock is glued to bottom.

Metal work can be filed on a wood lathe. Here, a block is screwed to faceplate to bear against leg of "lathe dog" that clamps around work with setscrew. When faceplate turns, block turns dog and dog turns work.

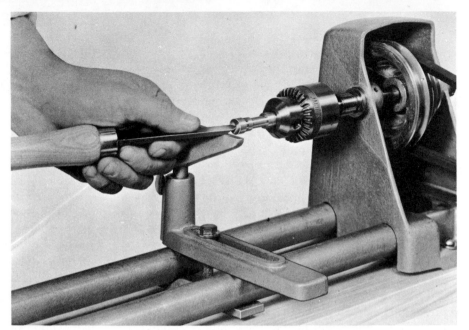

Freehand turning of soft metals is possible on wood lathe with carbide-tipped tools. This is not intended for precision work but for decorative projects like candlesticks.

The caliper is also very handy where a round tenon is being turned to fit a hole of specific size. The trick in using calipers is "feel." The caliper should be set so as to contact the surface with its tips, just slipping over it with very slight pressure. When it fits this way over the work it is matched to the pre-set dimension. If no example tenon is available for setting the caliper an inside caliper may be set to match the hole size, and the outside caliper set from that.

Accessories for the wood lathe include sanding disks, saw tables for circular saws to be mounted on the lathe spindle, and many others. In selecting a lathe look for one long enough "between centers" for the type of work you plan to do, and one that has enough "swing" for the diameter of the work. If a lathe can take a piece of wood 11″ in diameter and turn it on the spindle without scraping the lathe bed, it is called an 11″ lathe, or a lathe with an 11″ swing. Larger diameter work can be turned on the left-hand end of the headstock, where the work extends out beyond the end of the workbench where diameter is not limited by the swing or the height of the spindle above the bed.

Safety. The lathe is a comparatively safe tool to use if common sense is employed in the operation. It is particularly important in lathe work that no dangling clothing like neckties or loose cuffs be worn. The work revolving at high speed in the lathe can easily catch and wrap up such items and draw the operator violently into the work, causing very serious injury. It is important, also, to work gradually in roughing and general turning. A turning chisel thrust deeply into the work can sometimes cause the work to flip out of the lathe and toward the operator with dangerous force. The least it is likely to do is spoil the work. So take it easy. You'll find the job progresses with surprising rapidity even when the cuts are taken in very easy stages.

Diameter	Roughing Cuts	General Finish Cuts	Fine Finish and Sanding
Up to 2"	2072 r.p.m.	2700 r.p.m.	4000 r.p.m.
2" to 3"	1270	1270	2072
3" to 4"	805	1270	2072
4" to 5"	685	1270	1270
5" to 6"	685	805	1270
6" to 7"	500	805	1270
7" to 8"	500	685	805
8" to 9"	418	500	805
9" to 10"	418	500	685

These speeds are intended as an approximate guide only, and illustrate a range obtainable with a 1740 r.p.m. motor and typical drive system.

The Metalworking Lathe does the same type of work in metal that the wood lathe does in wood, but it's capable of much greater precision to suit the usual requirements of machine work. Its size is usually designated by the maximum diameter of the work it can handle. Many metalworking operations, however, can be done on large wood lathes for which metalworking accessories are available. But for the full range of metalwork, a lathe designed primarily for metal is usually required.

A compound slide rest holds the cutting bit. This rest consists of two slides, one above the other, that are moved along tracks by cranks that turn threaded shafts. On converted wood lathes, the compound rest is clamped to the lathe bed wherever required by the work, usually with the lower slide at right angles to the bed. The lower slide's feed crank can then be used to move the cutting

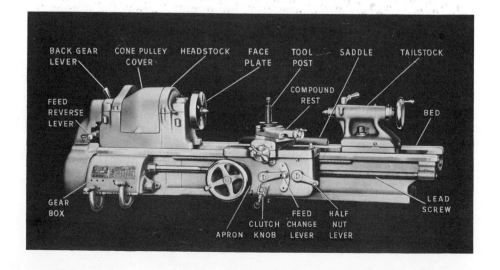

bit inward or outward to adjust the depth of cut. The upper slide's feed crank is used to move the bit lengthwise along the revolving work. The compound rest must be set accurately, according to the instructions for the lathe.

The Screw-Cutting Lathe is designed primarily for metal work. (The one shown is a 16" model made by South Bend Lathe, Inc., 400 West Sample Street, South Bend, Indiana 46621. Smaller lathes are also available.) Its compound rest is mounted on a carriage that consists of a saddle on top of the bed, and an apron in front. For screw cutting, the carriage is moved by a lead screw (pronounced *leed* screw). This is a threaded shaft mounted parallel to the bed, and as long as the working length of the bed. It works in the same manner as the feed crank screws in the slide rest, but is power driven. A gear-changing system at the lathe's headstock end lets you change the rate of carriage travel in relation to the r.p.m. of the spindle that turns the work, making it possible to cut a wide range of threads into the work. If, for example, the gears are set to move the carriage 1" along the bed while the work makes 8 revolutions, the tool bit will cut 8 threads per inch. Coarse threads result from slower carriage travel per revolution, finer threads from faster travel. Once the gears are set for a certain number of threads per inch, the ratio between spindle r.p.m. and carriage travel remains the same even though spindle r.p.m. is increased or decreased.

Tool bits are shaped according to the work they are designed to do and the metal they'll be cutting. Best bet for the beginner is to buy them readymade at first. With experience, you can grind your own from blanks.

Depth of cut depends on the lathe, the metal being cut, and the type of cutting operation. In general, roughing cuts to remove material and reduce work diameter can be up to $\frac{1}{16}$" deep in steel, reducing diameter $\frac{1}{8}$" on a typical converted wood lathe. Metal lathes for home shops can often handle about twice that depth; industrial lathes much more. But follow the instructions that come with the lathe you use. Finishing cuts are usually a little over $\frac{1}{100}$".

CHAPTER TWENTY-TWO

THE JOINTER

THE JOINTER is really a planing machine, often used to smooth edges and surfaces cut by a saw. The jointer does its work (called *jointing*) by means of a cylindrical cutter head in which the jointer knives (usually three) are mounted. Typically, the cutter head turns at about 3600 r.p.m. The size of the jointer is designated according to the length of its knives, as this determines the maximum board width that can be planed on it. The tool shown is made by American Machine & Tool Company, Inc., Royersford, PA. 19468.

Jointer

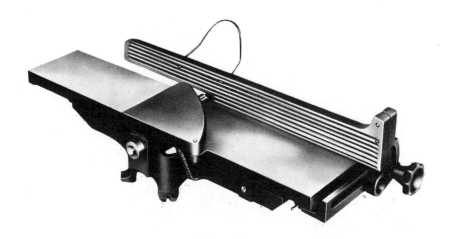

The jointer has two tables—a rear table that is adjusted exactly even with the cutting edges of the cutter knives, and a front table that is adjusted slightly lower to regulate the depth of cut. Thus, if the rear table is even with the revolving knife edges, and the front table is set ⅛″ lower, a board moved into the cutter head from the front table will be planed to a depth of ⅛″, and the planed surface will be even with the rear table.

The knives in the cutter head can be removed for sharpening. Different sharpening methods may be used, as long as the bevel angle of the cutting edge is maintained on each blade and the edge is kept straight. (A jig or a firm guide block is usually used.) Light cuts are then taken to avoid burning the edge, and all blades are ground in sequence to assure uniformity. The sharpened blades are then replaced and tightened so their cutting edges are again even and level with the rear table.

The guard covers the cutter head until it is pushed aside by the work passing over the head. Then the work, itself, covers the cutter head. Take the same precautions as with a power saw. Never feed the work into the cutter in such a way that a sudden slip could send your hands into the cutter. Also follow any additional precautions provided by the manufacturer.

The fence of the jointer can be moved across the table and locked in position, as on a table saw. Unlike a table-saw fence, however, it can be tilted at an angle to the table surface. The adjusting mechanism includes a protractor scale for this purpose. This enables you to smooth the edge of a board at any angle.

The jointer can also be used to plane across the end of a board (light cuts) if the board is short enough to handle safely. In this type of work, a backing block must be used. If a very wide board is to be edge-planed, a higher plywood fence can be attached to the original one to minimize the chance of tipping. The plywood is bolted to the original fence with flathead bolts, heads countersunk. Many jointers are made with holes in the fence for the bolts.

Truing cupped boards (convex on one surface, concave on the other) is easy on the jointer, as its tables are flat and the cutter knives straight and parallel with the table surfaces. The cupped board must be held firmly against the table, as level as possible, on its first pass through the cutter, which cuts a flat area on the cupped surface. Several passes may be required to complete each surface. Follow the same "uphill" rule given for hand planes on page 39. When surfacing thin wood (½″ or less) always use a wooden push block, *not your hands,* to move it into the cutter. The block should have a "step" in its under side so you can hold the work down and push it at the same time. A similar push block should be used on short pieces of work.

CHAPTER TWENTY-THREE

TOOLS FOR DELICATE WORK

Scroll Saw. This tool employs a narrow blade that reciprocates vertically through the center of a table.

The size is usually designated by the "throat" opening, the distance from the blade to the vertical part of the over arm. If this distance is 24″, the saw can cut to a depth of 24″.

Large saws can cut stock as thick as 2″. Small ones may be limited to less than an inch. Most scroll saws, however, are used in cutting intricate and ornate shapes in thin stock. The Dremel Moto-Saw shown has a 12″ throat capacity and can cut softwood up to 1½″ thick, hardwood to ¾″. The built-in 1.4-amp motor runs at 3450 r.p.m.

Scroll Saw

Hand Grinder

If the design to be cut is inside the edges of the material, you must bore a starting hole next to the cutting line (in waste material that will be removed), pass the blade through it, and mount the blade ends in the saw, a simple procedure. Then start the cut. As the blade is mounted to cut on the downstroke, it tends to hold the work on the table. You turn the work to cut the design.

Blades come coarse-toothed and fine, for cutting metal or wood.

Flexible Shaft Tools. These tools are especially suited for fine jewelry, models, and ornamental work. Bits available to fit them include burrs, minigrinders, saws, abrasive drums, cut-off wheels, and polishing wheels, in a wide variety of shapes. Some tools come with a variety of handpieces for working at angles and in small areas. One handpiece increases r.p.m. by a 2.7 to 1 ratio, from 25,000 to about 35,000 r.p.m. with the high-speed motor, up to 5000 or more when the cable is driven by a ¼″ power drill.

Hand Grinders. These do the same type of work as flexible shaft tools but are self-contained with a built-in motor turning at speeds up to 30,000 r.p.m. Use only accessories made for the tool and follow the manufacturer's instructions.

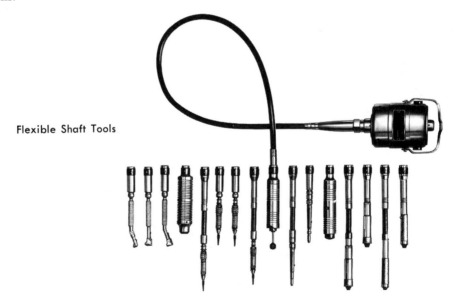

Flexible Shaft Tools

INDEX

A

Abrasives, choosing right grade, 81
Abrasives, plain sanding, 79
Abrasives, rounding corners, 79
Abrasives, sanding of carved work, 80
Abrasives, sanding techniques, 78–80
Abrasives, squaring corners, 80
Abrasives, table of, 78
Abrasives, types of, 77–81
Acrylic resin glue, 69
Adhesives, 69
Aliphatic resin glue, 69
Aluminum file, 66
Aluminum oxide paper, 77
Auger bit, 48–49
Awls, 46

B

Backsaw, 23, 24, 25
Ball joint disk, 108
Ball-peen hammer, 57–58
Band clamp, 75
Bandsaw blunt file, 65
Beading bit, 117
Belt sander, 110–111
Bevel cut, sabre saw, 98–99
Beveling, table saw, 121
Bit brace, 47
Bits, types of, 116–117
Black & Decker Co., 94
Blade teeth, sabre saw, 94–95
Blades, circular saw, 102–103
Blades, sabre saw, 94
Block plane, 41
Borden Co., 70
Boxwood rule, 12
Braces, types of, 47
Brad awl, 48
Brass file, 66
Breast drill, 46

Buna-n-Base adhesive, 72
Butcher, R. G. Dr., 7
Butcher saw, 7
Butt chisel, 31
Butt gauge, 21

C

Cabinet rasp, 66
Caliper rule, 12
Cantsaw file, 64, 65
C-clamp, 73
Cellulose nitrate cement, 70
Chisels, chamfering and trimming, 35
Chisels, how to make recess, 33–34
Chisels, metal-core handled, 32
Chisels, paring with, 35
Chisels, plastic-handled, 32
Chisels, sharpening and grinding, 35–37
Chisels, types of, 31–33
Chisels, wooden-handled, 32
Circular plane, 42
Circular saw, operations of, 101–105
Chamfering bit, 117
Clamps, types of, 73–76
Claw hammer, 10, 54, 57
Combination set, 17–18
Combination square, 17
Compass saw, 25
Contact cement, 70
Coping saw, 26
Core box bit, 117
Corner brace, 47
Corner clamp, 75
Corner cut, sabre saw, 100
Countersink, 52
Coving, radial-arm saw, 134
Coving, table saw, 123–124
Crosscut file, 65
Crosscut saw, 22–23, 24, 30
Crosscutting, circular saw, 104

Crosscutting, radial-arm saw, 131–132
Crosscutting, sabre saw, 96–97
Crosscutting, table saw, 124–125, 126
Curve cutting, sabre saw, 96
Curved-tooth file, 66
Cutting guides, sabre saw, 100

D

Depth gauges, 53
Depth of cut, sabre saw, 98
Disston D-38, 87
Double end bit, 117
Dovetail bit, 117
Dovetail saw, 25
Drill grinding, 49–51
Drill points, 53
Drill press, 137–143
Drill press, how to use, 138–139
Drill press, what it can do, 140–143
Drum sander, 109–110

E

Early tool lore, 7–11
Egyptian saws, 8
Emery paper, 77
Epoxy glue, 71
Even Flow Resin, 72
Expansive bit, 49–52
Extension rule, 12–13

F

Faceplate, wood lathe, 150
Fiberglass handle, 56
Files and rasps, types of, 63–66
Files, blade shapes, 64
Files, care of, 68
Files, coarseness of, 64
Files, curved tooth cut, 64
Files, double cut, 64
Files, how to use, 66–68
Files, rasp cut, 64
Files, single cut, 63–64
Firmer chisel, 9, 32

Flat file, 65, 66
Flexible shaft tools, 156
Flint paper, 77
Fore and jointer planes, 41
Forstner bit, 52
Framing chisel, 31
Framing square, 10, 18

G

Garnet paper, 77
Glues and clamps, types of, 69–76
Gouge chisel, 33
Grooving, radial-arm saw, 134
Grooving, table saw, 122–123

H

H. A. Calahan 3-Ton Adhesive, 69
Hacksaw, 26–27
Half-round file, 65, 66
Half-round shoe rasp, 66
Hammer stone, 9
Hammers, care of, 59
Hammers, how to use, 58–59
Hammers, judging quality of, 56–57
Hammers, types of, 54–57
Hand clamp, 73–75
Hand drills, types of, 45–49
Hand grinders, 156
Headstock, wood lathe, 149
Hickory handle, 54–55
Hide glue, 71
Hinge mortising bit, 116
Hole-making tools, 45–53
Hole saw, 7
Horse rasp, 66

I

International Paint Co., 72

J

Jack plane, 10, 41
Jointer, 153–154

K

Keyhole saw, 26

L

Lathe bed, wood lathe, 150
Lead float file, 66
Long angle lathe file, 66
Long cuts, circular saw, 104
Long-shank straight bit, 116

M

Magnetic hammer, 57
Marfix, 72
Masonry cutting, circular saw, 104–105
Metal-cutting blades, sabre saw, 95
Metal cutting, circular saw, 105
Metal lathe, 151–152
Mill chisel, 31
Mill files, 64–65
Millers Falls, 36, 94
Miter-box saw, 23, 24, 25
Miter cutting, table saw, 122
Modelmaker's plane, 42–43
Molding plane, 43
Mortise, 34
Multi-bore bit, 52–53

N

Nail hammer, curved claw, 54
Nail hammer, straight claw, 54

O

Offset screwdriver, 61
Ogee bit, 116
Orbital sander, 109

P

Panel bit, 117
Paring chisel, 31, 34
Pillar file, 66

Pitch, 19
Planes, care of, 43–44
Planes, how to use, 38–40
Planes, sharpening of, 44
Planes, types of, 38–44
Pliobond, 72
Plow plane, 41
Pocket chisel, 31
Pocket cuts, circular saw, 104
Polyester resin glue, 72
Polyvinyl acetate glue, 72
Portable circular saw, 101–105
Portable drill, circular saw attachment, 88–89
Portable drill, drill press attachment, 88
Portable drill, plane attachment, 89
Portable drill, sabre saw attachment, 88
Power drills, how to select, 91–92
Power drills, how to use, 90–91
Power drills, sanding attachments, 89–90
Power drills, types of, 86–88
Power sanders, 106–111
Power sanders, disk attachments, 107
Power tool shop, layout, 82–83
Power tool shop, location of, 84–85
Power tool shop, noise-cutting tips, 83–84
Power tool shop, planning of, 82–85
Power tool shop, walls and ceiling, 83
Precision hinging, sabre saw, 98
Push drill, 47

R

Rabbet plane, 41
Rabbeting bit, 117
Rabbeting, radial-arm saw, 134
Rabbeting, table saw, 123
Radial-arm saw, 130–136
Radial-arm saw, types of, 131
Reciprocating sander, 109
Resorcinol resin glue, 72–73
Rigid disk sander, 108
Ripping hammer, 10, 54
Ripping, radial-arm saw, 133
Ripping, sabre saw, 96–97
Ripping, table saw, 121
Ripsaw, 24–25, 30
Rise, 19

Round file, 65
Round-handle needle file, 66
Router, 112–117
Router guides, 113–114
Router, dado cut, 116
Router, groove cut, 116
Router, operating technique, 115–116
Routing, radial-arm saw, 135
Rubber-base adhesive, 73
Run, 19

S

Sabre saw, 93–100
Sanding, radial-arm saw, 135–136
Sandpaper, 10
Saw blades, 126–127, 128
Saws, care and sharpening of, 28
Saws, filing of, 30
Saws, setting teeth, 28–29
Saws, shaping teeth, 28
Saws, table of sharpening, 30
Saws, types of, 22–27
Scintilla, S.A., 93
Scratch awl, 47–48
Screw-cutting lathe, 151–152
Screwdriver bit, 62
Screwdrivers, cabinet blade, 60
Screwdrivers, grinding of blades, 62
Screwdrivers, keystone blade, 60–61
Screwdrivers, types of, 60–62
Screw-holding screwdriver, 62
Screws, use of, 62
Scroll saw, 155–156
Scrub plane, 41
Shamir stone, 10
Shaping, router, 114–115
Sharpening blades, 128–129
Shear-cut bit, 117
Skewbacked saw, 8
Short brace, 47
Silicon carbide, 11
Silicon carbide paper, 77
Simple rachet screwdriver, 62
Single end bit, 117
Sliding T-bevel, 18
Smooth plane, 41
Soft-face hammer, 57
South Shaftsbury, Vermont, 10
Span, 19

Squares, 15–18
Square file, 65
Spindle, wood lathe, 149
Spiral ratchet screwdriver, 62
Spokeshave, 42
Spring clamp, 75
Spur center, wood lathe, 149
Stair routing bit, 117
Stanley Tool Co., 12, 14, 17, 75
Stationery power tools, 82–83
Steel handle, 55–56
Steel tape rule, 13–14
Straight-backed saw, 8
Straight bit, 117
Straight deep-cutting bit, 116
Surform tool, 43

T

Table saw, 118–125
Tailstock, wood lathe, 150
Taper cutting, table saw, 124
Taper file, 65
Taper ground blade, 23
Thor-Speedway, 92
Three-square file, 65
Titebond, 69
Tools for measuring and marking, 12–21
Try and miter square, 17
Try square, 15
Twist drill, 49

V

Vermont Marble Co., 72
"V" grooving bit, 116

W

Warding file, 66
Weldwood Super Contact Cement, 70
Whimble brace, 47
Wing divider, 14
Wood lathes, 144–145
Wood marking gauge, 21
Wood rasp, 66

Z

Zig-Zag rule, 12